MARY'S PLAN

The Madonna Comes to Santa Maria

MARY'S PLAN

The Madonna Comes to Santa Maria

by
J. Ridley Castro

The publisher recognizes and accepts that the final authority regarding the apparitions at Santa Maria rests with the Holy See of Rome, to whose judgment we willingly submit.

The Publisher

Cover art and design:
    Janet Schaefer

Copyright ©1993 Queenship Publishing

Library of Congress Catalogue No. 93-083223

ISBN: 1-882972-08-2

Printed in the United States of America

Dedication

*To The Immaculate Heart of Mary
That she may bless this work, initiated
during the Advent of the Triumph*

and

*To Barbara Matthias
That Our Lady of the Immaculate Heart
may always safeguard Barbara in the
Heart of the Holy Trinity*

Acknowledgments

No endeavor is completed without the assistance of many people. I can not begin to express my gratitude to my husband Bob and my family who patiently supported me throughout this writing.

For all of the priests who offered their Mass intentions, I am thankful. Their prayers sustained me spiritually. I am also grateful in a very special way to Fr. Luke Zimmer, Fr. Richard Culver, Fr. Bernard Massicotte, Monsignor John Rohde and Fr. Rene Laurentin.

Anna Marie Maagdenberg assisted me in compiling the scientific data presented in this work. It would have been impossible to summarize the reports without her assistance.

Without the help of John and Barbara Gayton and Rosie and Eddie Bernardo this book would have taken many more months to complete. Their assistance on all fronts brought the work to the press.

And , finally, I would like to acknowledge Barbara Matthias, who cooperated throughout the past two years — humbly, cheerfully and meritoriously. May her life be eternally filled with the Joy of the Holy Family.

Author's Note

The purpose of this book is to introduce the reader to a community of faithful Christians who have been invited to help Our Lady carry out a plan: a plan for the transition of hearts, a plan for living the Gospel life, a plan of action and obedience, a plan of triumph and peace. It is also the presentation of facts about the visionary Barbara Matthias and her initial messages received from the Holy Virgin during the apparitions. The messages give us a further insight into Mary's Plan for Santa Maria and Peace in the world. It is a story of blessings, purifications and faith, as well as struggles, trials and adversity.

I was encouraged to pursue writing this text by friends, scientists, and priests but most of all by the good Christian people in Santa Maria who for many years have dedicated their lives to Our Lord and His Blessed Mother.

The work was a difficult task. I spent five years gathering information and six years researching mystical phenomena. During the most important phase of this endeavor it was a great privilege for me to have the opportunity to work with the world renown Marian theologian, Fr. Rene Laurentin of Paris, who I believe will one day become a Doctor of the Church. Over the course of two years I spent many days and many hours with him. He constantly pressed me for precision in documenting everything as best as possible and taught me to openly approach the complexities and conflicts that have surrounded the events in Santa Maria.

I am also thankful for the wisdom and insight of Dr. Mark Miravalle, Professor of Theology at the University of Steubenville in Ohio. There were times I felt like giving up, and had it not been for his encouragement and discernment I might have done so.

I was constantly submerged in books and paperwork which caused some people to label me as an intellectual. This surprised me because I don't see myself in that light at all. I will admit to being a searcher: one who questions, one who seeks to discover truth and one who tries to find solutions to complex problems. In the process of this research and documentation I have discovered that the saying, "the more you think you know, the more you don't know", seems to ring true. It is also true that a single work can not be totally definitive when so many facets of an event exist.

I love people, and I'm interested in how they see themselves, how they see others, and how they search and long for God in their lives. I also have a great passion for helping those who are handicapped in one way or another, especially those who are misunderstood; those who cry out to be heard and those who are victims of a society that has by in large lost love.

At the age of 52, I can truly say I have been blessed by God. I have been married to the same wonderful man for 31 years. He is a kind, devout man who has given his life to me forever on this earth. I am also a mom to three beautiful children: a son and two daughters who are now grown and succeeding in their vocations. A great joy in my life is my two year old grandson who has a smile that will melt any heart. Sadly, my intact family structure has become a minority statistic in today's American society as so many families are caught up in our secular culture where worldly influences lead to the destruction of the family unit.

Suffering has also touched my life in many ways. I nearly died three times and have known what it is like to grow up in a one parent family. Several years ago I permanently injured my back so my physical abilities have been limited. Jesus tells us that suffering makes us strong so I have learned to focus on the good side of life by abandoning myself to God and living each moment as it arrives.

My medical background comes from being an operating room surgical technician in my younger days. I have recently retired from the field of Special Education where I worked with the handicapped for the past 16 years. Between the former and the latter I was the Executive Director of the Idaho Park Foundation. So, you might say I've had a "potluck" of occupations that placed me in a framework of many enlightening and fascinating experiences.

As a lay minister in the Catholic Church for the past 13 years I served as a parish prayer group leader, seminar teacher, speaker, spiritual counselor and minister in the federal prison system.

I have been under the guidance of a personal spiritual director for 12 years. He is an order priest whose background is rooted in scripture, sound theology and prayer. He is also a mystic that is highly gifted by God in the areas of wisdom, knowledge and discernment. He is firm in directing me and I am very thankful for being able to receive the benefit of his acumen and insights.

Now that you know something about me I will return to the intent of this book. It is simply a prelude, primarily the early history of the faith community in

Santa Maria and the presentation of a unique woman named Barbara, who since March of 1990, is a recipient of daily apparitions and a messenger of Our Lady's invitation to seek our eternal home in Heaven. But the chronicle is not without controversy and conflicts which seem to be part of any apparition story.

For the past three years her messages have been in a discernment process by a team of priests, religious sisters, theologians and lay people. Her state of ecstasy and psychological equilibrium have been studied scientifically by world experts. It is not pathological nor is she faking or pretending to see Our Lady of the Immaculate Heart.

A detailed account of the independent theological investigations and scientific tests is not the main focus of this particular writing; however, the *positive results* have paved the way for this volume and the release of her initial messages. Other publications will parallel and follow this first endeavor.

I have attempted to acquaint the reader with the events as I know them, and it is an earnest effort to relate the necessary facts as simply as possible.

J. Ridley Castro
March 25, 1993

Table of Contents

Chapter 1 - Early Dawn 1

Chapter 2 - Mid-Morning 13

Chapter 3 - High Noon 19

Chapter 4 - Afternoon 23

Chapter 5 - Mid-Day 29

Chapter 6 - Late Afternoon 35

Chapter 7 - Another Time Zone 43

Chapter 8 - A Time for Change 47

Chapter 9 - Half Past Four 55

Chapter 10 - Hours of Confusion 63

Chapter 11 - Hours of Grave Trial 69

Chapter 12 - Dinner Time 79

Chapter 13 - A Time for Discerning 85

Chapter 14 - Hours of Freedom and Change 91

Chapter 15 - Scientific Twilight Zone 93

Chapter 16 - The Hour for Bringing Believers Together 105

Chapter 17 - A Time to Plan and Understand 121

Chapter 18 - Infinite Moments 125

Chapter 19 - Awaiting a New Dawn 133

Publishers Preface to the Messages 139

Messages 141

Chapter 1

Early Dawn

A reflection on Genesis 1:1-8 is how many people relate to the place they call home — Santa Maria. At a personal level it might be something like this:

In the beginning God created the Santa Maria Valley. He created the sun, the moon, and the stars that shine upon this wonderful place. But at first it was formless: no scenic hills with green vegetation, no animals, no roads, no houses, no human beings, no society. He situated Santa Maria near the vast Pacific Ocean on the Central Coast of California, and His Divine Wind (Spirit) swept over the water. Then God divided light from darkness in this valley and permitted His radiance to illuminate all that had existed in obscurity. Evening came and morning came; the first day dawned.

There is a deep sense of beholding God's creation and His presence here. The people appreciate the beauty of the valley and are very thankful for all of God's blessings upon the land.

When you talk to the residents, they will tell you they believe the Santa Maria Valley is an exceptional area. How do they know? They simply sense it — it's something perceived deep within their spirits. "There is just a special Peace here," they say.

I'm sure that most people have hometown pride, and we all know that some areas of this immense earth have a rather mystical, natural splendor. Santa Maria is not a metropolis of perfect people living in a "Garden of Eden". It has its share of urban problems just like many other U. S. cities. However, it is a dedicated community of citizens who care deeply about the quality and equality of life. There is a great Christian faith and an ecumenical spirit among the people. Churches are full on Sunday mornings.

Visitors to the city are welcomed in a typical "Santa Maria Style" of congenial hospitality. In fact, ever since the mid 1800's Santa Maria has been famous for the Santa Maria Style Bar-B-Que that sizzles on street corner pits almost every weekend. Service organizations, church groups and youth sport teams have all become adept at building the special oak pit fire and seasoning the meat for a superb flavor. Those who travel through the city will usually remember the appetizing aroma of the Barb-B-Que wafting in the air.

Santa Maria is located 170 miles north of Los Angeles in Santa Barbara County. The population of the valley is 104,600 with 64,046 people living within the city limits. [*Santa Maria Valley Chamber of Commerce, 1992 census*] Surrounding the city one can see rolling hills and vast areas of rich farm land that produce everything from broccoli to flowers to pinquito beans. A refreshing breeze sweeps off the ocean to the west keeping the atmosphere clean and clear. Near perfect day time temperatures of 70 degrees predominate almost year round. When the wind gusts, I often hear the good-natured Christians quip, "The Holy Spirit is blowing today," or "The Blessed Mother is present; her sign is the wind."

A Little History

Aside from prehistoric times the first people to live in the Santa Maria Valley were the Chumash Indians. How did they arrive? No one knows for sure but they must have discovered refuge here when trying to escape severe conditions elsewhere. One must surmise that when they discovered this valley they felt at home, inspired by its beauty and potential for growing food. It was Juan Rodriguez Cabrillo who first met the Chumash nearly 50 years after Columbus had reached the eastern part of our continent. [Santa Maria Valley Historical Society, *This is Our Valley* p. 2]

The book *This is Our Valley,* gives an account of how the Santa Maria River was named.

> *Fuflot de Mofras, reporting on his travels along the coast in 1842, referred in this fashion to the Santa Maria River: 'The eighteen leagues that separate the Mission de la Concepcion from that of San Luis Obispo consist primarily of an extensive plain called La Larga. This land, watered by the San Geraldo River, is noted for its fine grazing.'*
>
> *Don Juan Pacifico Ontiveros is credited with having named the river, his rancho and the nearby mesa after Mary, Mother of Jesus — Santa Maria. [Ibid., p.4]*

Like all towns, the city of Santa Maria had its first day and its first settlers from the east. For a brief time it was called Grangerville, finally being named Central City in 1874. The four founding fathers Cook, Miller, Fesler and Thornburgh each donated 40 acres of land to establish the city and the central point where each parcel converged became the center of the town. [*Ibid.,* p. 48-49]

Again, in the book, *This is Our Valley*, a declaration is made regarding the name being changed to Santa Maria — the Spanish spelling of Holy Mary.

> The change of name from Central City to Santa Maria, was noted in the first issue of the **Santa Maria Times**, dated April 22, 1882, H. J Laughlin, proprietor; S. Clevenger, editor and manager.
>
> Postmasters of the United States were having trouble with the old name, the editor declared; and mail meant for this growing town was being sent to Central City, Colorado.
>
> 'If the post office name cannot be changed,' the Times said, 'then the name of the town should be. If...Santa Maria is to be the name of the place, our citizens should take immediate steps to establish that fact.'
>
> (Oddly, the legal commission of S. J. Lockwood, first postmaster, named him 'postmaster of Santa Maria,' according to the old document in the possession of Gaylord Jones.) [Ibid., p.117]

Was this a providential circumstance? Did Our Lady softly whisper her name in the ears of that legal commission years ago? Everyone is free to believe what they want, but hundreds of Christians who live here discretely believe this was all a part of the Lord's plan for the Santa Maria Valley.

The region, located on the El Camino Real (US Highway 101) between Mission Santa Ynez and Mission San Luis Obispo, has no doubt received its rich religious heritage from the days when Father Serra trekked through California pounding small Crosses in the ground on the spots where he wanted to establish Missions. The geological maps show how many areas bear the name of Our Lady and the Saints. The

Franciscan missionaries certainly must have blessed the land and left it for the Saints to "watch over".

Today three Catholic parishes serve the immediate Santa Maria area: St. Mary of the Assumption, St. Louis de Montfort and St. John Neumann. Two Catholic elementary schools and one high school provide Catholic education for students.

The Prayer Groups

The Central Coast from Monterey to Santa Barbara is alive with vibrant prayer groups and small "faith communities". They meet in parishes, monasteries, seminaries, novitiates, schools, homes and even a park. There are charismatic prayer groups, Bible study prayer groups, youth prayer groups, contemplative prayer groups and Rosary prayer groups. Some are large and some are small, but each provides spiritual enrichment for those who participate. Every day of the week there is a group centered in prayer seeking the Lord Jesus Christ, interceding for peace and the salvation of all mankind.

The parishes in Santa Maria all have prayer groups that meet either at the church or in homes. They are well established and center their prayer on Jesus in the Eucharist. The Blessed Mother has always been honored with devotion and love in these groups who unite to serve and strengthen the heart of each parish.

Early Prophecies Documented

When I first became one of the core leaders in the St. Louis de Montfort prayer group in 1980, I heard many extraordinary stories of how people came to live in Santa Maria. They seemed to confirm the same extraordinary way my husband and I came to live here. I also heard about the "early prophecies" that had been given for the Central Coast of California and the Santa Maria Valley. What impressed me was the profound belief the group had: they were earnestly following a divine call of preparation given to them.

It was not until autumn of 1989 that I seriously began to research these early prophecies. It was finally through Fr. Michael Cicinato, Pastor of Nativity of Our Lady Catholic Church in San Luis Obispo, that I found my answer. I was also to find that if I had tried any earlier I probably would not have been successful because Fr. Cicinanto had only recently returned to the area after being absent for a number of years.

In October I paid him an unannounced visit. He was knee deep in the activities of his diocese (Monterey Diocese), so I had really caught him at an inopportune time. We chatted briefly and he assured me he would help me out. On November 7, 1989, he sent me a letter (with a copy to Monsignor John Rohde and G. Patrick Ziemann, Auxiliary Bishop of the Los Angeles Diocese) detailing the prophecies now published in this book for the first time.

"...We have reviewed the records we have of the prophecies during that period, including the prophecies and teachings given at the Santa Maria Day of Unity

sometime between November 1976 and March 1977. What follows is the result of our research, prayer and sharing.

The scriptures, teachings and prophecies of that time echo a call for the <u>people</u> of the Central Coast to be a 'light on the mountain top' and a 'beacon of refuge for the world'. The prophecies point out that 'many will come from the north and the south to find refuge and solace here.' We, The People of God were called to be that refuge. We were called to give spiritual, moral <u>and physical</u> sustenance to those who come.

We were called to prepare for difficult times to come. There was also a clear call to confront sin in our lives — sin visible in our government, educational and economic structures. We are especially called to see the sin in our Church and to seek healing and forgiveness. The call was to confront sin with the truth of Jesus — not just preached, but <u>lived!</u>

On the Day of Unity the call to the people of Santa Maria was a call to lay down their <u>lives,</u> to be willing to wash feet and even to die in all areas of their lives for the Lord. This call to death was especially to die to personal ambition and preconceived ideas. It was a call based on much listening to Jesus.

God was understood to be speaking a clear word to people that involved people — <u>not</u> <u>structures</u>. It was a call to be ready to move as a People of God. It was a call to be fluid in the hands of the Lord as a community, not just as 'like-minded charismatics.' It would also include laying down our lives even for those who are antagonistic, and being willing to serve by '<u>feeding, clothing,</u> and <u>sheltering.</u>'

Preparation for all this was to involve 'learning how to love as brothers and sisters through prayer, witness of the Word, and shared life.' The shared life, involved most especially — being built around the Eucharist — God made present through the gathering together, the Word proclaimed and lived, and the Body and Blood of Jesus shared.

The above sharing and teaching was meant to be for the whole Central Coast. There was a <u>specific</u> call for the 'Church of Santa Maria' to come together to pray and discern, a coming together which transcended the divisions at the time. Mutual discernment, based on sound teaching, was not an option, but a <u>'must'</u>. Responding to God's Word was a priority, not a luxury. Support and submission to leaders (Church community) was a must. Discerning and measuring leadership by gifts manifested was essential in the prayer groups (not just choosing strong personalities or popular, vocal people). The call involved learning how to forgive and to make clear agreements.

Involvement with Church leaders in specific ways was shared. The emphasis of this teaching was to love them, without trying to change them; to pray for them, especially for their homilies and teaching. It reminded the community of the need to not beat leaders over the head with scriptures or witness — these were God's sword, not ours. People were called to expect God to work through their leaders.

I have dwelt extensively on the Day of Unity because that day was specifically for Santa Maria. The teaching and prophecy that day, however, were reflections of the continuing call that we received over the three year period (from 1976-1978) for the whole Central Coast.

My sense, and that of the leaders and members I was able to contact, is clear that the call was to build a people...The people were to be a light and a beacon through the way they lived and shared the love of Jesus in 'concrete' ways, particularly with those who might seek refuge or help here. Difficult times ahead were foreseen, which would send people here for various kinds of help, and God's people here were to be ready to help..." [Letter from Rev. Michael Cicinato, Pastor, Our Lady of the Nativity, November 7, 1989]

The early history of Montfort Family Prayer Group was one of patient suffering. When the group began in the mid seventies they were not allowed to meet on Church property. It seemed that the awakening of the charisms was not welcomed by the local clergy so the group met at St. Joseph High School and was joined by parishioners from St. Mary's.

The leaders told me that during this time a visiting nun gave a prophecy which they all remember quite vividly. She prophetically said that the Lord had called them to have a teaching ministry and that the effects of their teaching would be known world wide. This stunned the group but they listened with enthusiasm. When I asked them what happened to the nun, they said they never saw her again; and over the years no one has been able to locate her.

Action of the Holy Spirit

They continued to pray, wait, and discern the will of the Holy Spirit. What evolved was an eventual permission by Fr. Anthony Runtz, the new pastor of St. Louis de Montfort, for the group to meet each Thursday in the new parish hall. Fr. Anthony (a Josephite Father) had been the acting Associate Pastor of St. Mary's and was given the assignment as Pastor of St. Louis de Montfort in 1975. It was also at this time that the Josephite Order petitioned the Archdiocese of Los Angeles for permission to take over the parish duties of St. Louis de Montfort. As time passed Fr. Anthony became a great supporter of the prayer group, encouraging their prayer life, charisms and ministries.

Fr. Anthony, a skilled carpenter like St. Joseph, brought about many changes in parish life during the time he was pastor. He initiated the construction of a new parish hall, rectory and playground at the school; reformed the parish council; started parish renewal week-ends; and established Eucharistic Ministers. But most profoundly, he encouraged and nurtured a deep spiritual renewal in the people he pastored. Thus, the Holy Spirit began to move in a powerful way.

In 1979 the parish prayer group united with SCRC (Southern California Renewal Communities) which had formed under the direction of the late Fr. Ralph Tischenor, S.J. The leaders spent a number of years absorbed in deep spiritual formation, developed a solid a leadership through SCRC, and served on Area Pastoral Teams. Ultimately, the group was ready to launch the teaching ministry they had been called to establish through the nun's prophecy.

They began to conduct Holy Spirit Seminars twice a year at the parish level and then in surrounding communities. The fruits were abundant as people were having deep transformations of heart. The parishes were coming alive almost like the times of St. Paul and the infant Christian Church. This spiritual awakening moved like a mighty wind igniting a fire of faith and prayer, healings and conversions. As a result various ministries developed bringing Christians together in fellowship, unity and love.

Most of the local clergy observed the manifestation of the Spirit but took a fundamental line of prudence. Many of the priests were not open to the explosion of charisms; and at one point, all that they could do was tolerate this dynamite renewal among the laity. Their greatest fear was that they might have a bunch of fanatics on their hands. It was a tremendous anguish for many of the parishioners, but they kept the flame alive by persevering in prayer. Sensitivity and respect of the clergy was important, and over the years the fruit of obedience was balance and stability. But Satan was strong, and he stepped up his attacks constantly trying to divide and conquer. At times he would win a battle but never the war. Those who were lost were finding Christ, and those who were lukewarm were being revitalized.

The prophecies continued. Discretely and judiciously the prayer group discerned, waiting quietly with expectant faith. When the rest of the world was putting The Blessed Mother in the background, this parish prayer group was always renewing its consecration to her. The leaders never started a core meeting without first praying the Rosary and every prayer meeting ended with a Hail Mary.

On April 19, 1985, one of the leaders, a young man in his thirties, received this locution from Jesus:

> "...There is a need for much intercessory prayer...there is still much preparation that needs to be done. The battle is being fought now, but the victory is almost complete...I will settle for no less than total victory in Santa Maria. When I enthrone My Mother as Queen of the Valley, all will come to believe. The enemy will be defeated, and the valley will shine as a beacon for the whole world to see. All those who don't believe in the role and power that has been given to My Mother will believe..." [Records, Montfort Prayer Group, 1988.]

Did these words indicate an eventual significant presence of the Blessed Mother here? Time would tell.

Then on April 28, 1985, he received another locution from Jesus, but this time only for the core leaders of the prayer group.

> *"There is much to be done. You must act now in bringing others into the leadership so they will be ready when I call all of you to the work of another apostolate. When you bring them in, you must let them know that they will be assuming a leadership role. Then all of you will step down. It is not necessary for you to tell them why at this time, only that I have called you to another ministry. You will also be intercessors of prayer. You must all commit yourselves totally to Me...Do not concern yourselves with the negative things that will go on around you. Root yourselves in Me keeping your eyes focused on My light and I will prevail..."* [Records, Montfort Prayer Group, 1985]

The messages were sent to the Spiritual Director (and later to the Regional Bishop) while at the same time discretely guarded by the leadership.

The leaders prayed and discerned. As Jesus had asked, the next three years were spent quietly training a new group of people who could assume the ministry. They patiently awaited the Lord's call to step down as parish prayer group leaders.

By 1986 the Regional Bishop B. Patrick Ziemann taught sessions in several Holy Spirit seminars. He was pleased with the teaching ministry the prayer group had established and encouraged the spiritual renewal he observed among the participants.

Chapter 2

Mid-Morning

In the spring and fall of 1987 Charlie and Carol Nole (the Cross of Peace locutionist) attended their first Holy Spirit Seminars at St. Louis de Montfort Church. Charlie said, "They were disappointed that they hadn't received any special gifts such as prophecy or discernment, or at least it didn't appear that they had at the time. Later Carol's gift would flow." [*Cross of Peace Messenger*, First Quarter 1990]

In October of 1987 Charlie and Carol began acquainting the prayer group and the community at large with Our Lady's apparitions in Medjugorje. At the same time they started coming to the prayer group leadership training meetings on a weekly basis but never became core group leaders.

Carol is a very thin, soft spoken woman in her fifties, with a heartwarming expression in her eyes and gentle smile. Her accommodating, docile demeanor is a vivid contrast to her husband Charlie, who is witty, zealous and gifted with astute organizational skills and boundless energy.

The Local Clergy Responds to Medjugorje

News of Medjugorje was met with mixed reactions. Most of the people in the prayer group were interested and wanted to have as much information as possible. Despite the fact that millions of people including priests and bishops had witnessed spiritual conversion and renewal in Medjugorje, once again the local clergy, holding its fundamental line of conservatism, did not want any videos or talks given about these happenings at any Catholic Church in Santa Maria. And once again, obedience by the laity was observed.

When pilgrimages to the small Yugoslavian village continued to increase, Charlie and Carol and several other people in Santa Maria had a great desire to make the pilgrimage. My husband and I shared this desire. We wanted to experience what was happening there first hand.

Carol Nole's Surprise

On March 24, 1988, Carol received the first inner locution from Our Lady. The message was preparatory: *"You will go; do not worry. You will be great couriers for me."* [Charles and Carol Nole, *A Cross Will Be Built...* p. 3.]*

Subsequently, their finances were arranged and plans were made to go for the June 24, 1988, anniversary of Medjugorje.

Much to Carol's surprise on April 9, 1988, (the first Sunday after Easter) she received another locution from the Blessed Virgin: a request for a Cross to be built on a hill on the north side of town.

Perhaps it is significant that Carol received the message for building the Cross on the very Sunday that Jesus had specified to Sister M. Faustina (to be beatified April 18, 1993), in February of 1931 as the Sunday He wanted to be celebrated in the universal

---

* *All messages received through Carol Nole are quoted from "A Cross will be Built".*

Church as the Feast of Mercy. [Diary of Sr. M. Faustina Kowalska, *Divine Mercy in My Soul*, #49, p. 24.] This feast has yet to be designated by the Holy See.

Charlie and Carol gave the messages to the leadership of the prayer group. What should she do? The leaders advised them of a need for discernment and asked them to wait and see if Carol would receive any more messages. They also cautioned them about discretion, advising them that the clergy may not be open to Carol's religious experiences.

The group was puzzled about the location of the hill and began to look on the north side of town. It was a mystery. But on April 19, 1988, she received another message: a request for a specific design of the Cross with a height of 75 feet. The message also said, *"Go forth, do not wait. I have told you where it is to be built...You know where it is to be built. Follow my instructions exactly."* In jest, everyone thought that either the Blessed Mother or Carol might be having a problem with geography. Where on the north side of town was the Cross to be built?

The next day April 20, 1988, The Holy Virgin said to Carol, *"Do not worry, the size is important that all may see. Many will come and many will stay in my City of Peace."* She was saying don't worry! That was easy for Our Lady the group thought, but what about the location? The search for the hill intensified. Special maps were obtained and the frustration continued. By now a few other people in the prayer group were aware of the message and search for the hill. Finally, Carol was requested to pray and ask for more specific directions from the Blessed Virgin. Everyone waited in suspense. Five days later on April 28, 1988, the answer came: *"Seek and you shall find. Take the Canyon road to find the area where the two paths intersect. There will sit the Cross.*" This made things a little easier, and several days later Charlie said that he had discovered there was only one place where the Canyon Road (Bull Canyon) intersected on the north side of town. It was at highway 166.

Discovery of the Hill

Plans were immediately made to meet Charlie and Carol on a Saturday morning at the intersection of Bull Canyon Road and Highway 166. After arriving, everyone (a group of 10 or so) proceeded to climb a rugged hill closest to the intersection. It was an old rock quarry (later to become quite significant) and did not seem suitable for the erection of a 75 foot Cross.

The group prayed but only received a sense that they did not have the correct hill. Then suddenly one of the women named Janet Real turned and pointed to a hill to the west of where everyone was standing. *"There it is,"* she yelled, as she took off running with an extraordinary speed toward the other hill. Shouts of caution came from the others who watched with amazement. Right below her were six mean looking bulls grazing in the pasture. *"Never mind,"* she said, *"Our Lady will make them flee."* She was right; they fled like docile little lambs, disappearing over a small knoll.

The others quickly followed two by two, but widely separated. Each pair experienced an intense heat radiating intermittently from the ground as they traversed the 1500 foot hill. But this intense heat was only discussed between each of the two who were ascending the terrain together. It was not until everyone reached the crest of the hill that they discovered they had all experienced the same phenomenon. As it was a very cool day, everyone thought this might be a sign from Our Lady.

Kneeling on the ground, the small band of Mary's children began the Glorious Mysteries of the Rosary seeking a confirmation through prayer. During the Our Fathers and the Hail Marys the air became unduly still, but with each Gloria the wind blew with a blast. Was this another sign from the Blessed Virgin?

To mark the spot, the group scrambled to find some large rocks and lay out a Cross on the ground. Each rugged stone was placed with prayer and care to form the flat, horizontal symbol of Salvation. The vision of an eventual tall, vertical 75 foot Cross danced in the imagination of each person's head. According to Our Lady, this Cross was to be different — no corpus, just the nail holes where light could shine through golden stained glass. The Cross was also to be a remembrance for all of her children, *to give them hope and peace in their hearts. Mankind has forgotten God, who loves us,* she had said.

The valley was beautiful that day. One could see for miles. The sparkling Pacific Ocean lay to the west; lush grape vineyards and rolling farm land surrounded the hill; the city of Santa Maria nestled in the distance below.

From that time on, Carol never received another message about the site, so it was presumed that the correct hill had been located.

Another Response from the Clergy

During this same time frame, and unknown to the rest of the group who had advised caution, Charlie went to see Fr. G. Garcia, pastor of St. Louis de Montfort, about the locutions Carol was receiving from Our Lady. Fr. Garcia had assumed his duties as pastor in 1985, following in the footsteps of Fr. Runtz. He was not receptive, refused to read the messages and immediately suggested the entire matter be taken to the Regional Bishop. This type of refusal can be a disappointment to any individual and a definite sense of abandonment, because the Vatican Council II Document on the Laity has expressly instructed pastors to discern the charisms experienced by the people. On the other hand, bishops and the clergy are mindful of Scripture which says, *Leave them alone, for if this plan and work of theirs is a man-made thing, it will disappear; but if it comes from God you cannot possibly defeat them. Take care not to find yourselves fighting against God.* [Acts 5:38-39. NJB] The clergy is also attentive to *Lumen Gentium* (#66-67) which serves to remind The People of God that a balanced attitude must be maintained towards the place of special cults in our devotional life.

It was a dilemma. If the clergy refused to give immediate direction, what would the result be? Would it eventually leave the entire project vulnerable to trials, confusion, disunity and possible scandal? Carol Nole seemed to be in a "Catch 22" situation. But this is nothing new in the life of the Church. This type of phenomenon has always been at the very bottom of the priority list. Again obedience was followed.

Chapter 3

High Noon

A Call for Resignation

On May 1, 1988, the Montfort prayer group core leaders received a directive from the Lord (A Word of Wisdom given to one of the leaders through prayer) that the time had come for them to step down from their positions.

> *Begin with the Novena to the Holy Spirit as directed by My Mother, Queen of Peace for the whole world...You will gather before me present in the tabernacle in the chapel at Marian Hospital. You will remain once each day in prayer for nine days. I will pour forth, through My Mother, all the graces you will need to sustain your task. It will not be easy, as many will reject you in the beginning; but My Mother's Immaculate Heart will, in the end, triumph.*
>
> *On the Feast of Pentecost (1988) you will resign from your leadership positions in the prayer group and begin to spread my message of love, repentance, conversion, fasting, prayer and penance for the wounds inflicted by mankind against my Sacred Heart. Humanity has wounded me in continual disobedience to my words proclaimed in the Gospels. You must teach those who have been blinded by the plans of Satan. Pray much and you will see the work of my hands through you. You must remain in the unity of the Heart of the Holy Family, for you will see many blessings in your work for family unity. Peace begins with each of you, then to families. This is my call to you, and all that you*

do is to be united to my Eucharistic Heart in each Mass celebrated throughout time.

Do not worry for my call to you is a moment of grace. Thank you for listening to the Sorrows of My Heart. [Records, Montfort Prayer Group, 1988.]

The resignation was submitted to Fr. Garcia several days later.

Most of the core leaders had served for at least ten years. To this day, the original group of eight have continued to work towards Our Lady's plans being fulfilled; and they also unite in intercessory prayer for these intentions.

They offered their sufferings as well: the death of one leader; the near death of one couple's premature baby; two leaders suffered heart attacks; another leader had open heart surgery and suffered 3 strokes, one that resulted in a permanent partial blindness; another leader suffered kidney failure, eventually went on dialysis for 13 months, and then received a kidney transplant; another leader had a balloon angioplasty of his heart arteries; and two leaders suffered debilitating injuries. Yet, during all of these sufferings, they remained active in ministry — even from their hospital beds. Their healings amazed the community, and some seem to be an extraordinary grace from God.

One core leader attended college full time, then entered the seminary and was ordained to the priesthood (at age 65) October 24, 1992, at St. Louis de Montfort Church. He is now serving in the Society of Our Lady of the Most Holy Trinity in Belen, New Mexico.

On May 13, 1988, the group, including Charlie and Carol Nole, began the nine day Novena to the Holy Spirit at Marian Hospital, meeting each day in prayer before the tabernacle as the Lord had asked. It was difficult because of work schedules, but no one missed the days of prayer and penance.

Chapter 4

Afternoon

The Perplexing Problem

Having faith and trust challenges our weak human natures, especially when all that is taking place is believed to be directed by divine providence. How could the site selected by Our Lady be obtained from the Newhall Land and Farming Company? On May 14, 1988, the Virgin had said to Carol *"call on the land, it is important."*

Contact was eventually made with the foreman of the ranch. He was friendly, interested and cautious. For many weeks he had allowed the small group to come privately for prayer on the top of the hill. Those were marvelous days and a great privilege for all who gathered at the foot of the stone Cross. One had the feeling of ascending the mount like Moses, who interceded before God for his people.

It was through the foreman that the group ultimately heard an astonishing story about the rock quarry (the original hill they had climbed). Many years prior the foreman had excavated rocks from the quarry and taken them to St. Mary of the Assumption Church for construction of a grotto honoring Our Lady. The grotto located on the north side of the Church, facing the hill, is still a special place for prayer. Certainly this could be another sign confirming the Blessed Mother's plans, thought everyone.

But what should be done? Could the foreman of the ranch be of help? His suggestion was to correspond with the land owners.

On May 19, 1988, Our Lady said to Carol, *"...Every day meditate and pray and my plan will flow into each heart that is to be touched that day. My children, not even you can conceive the beauty of what will be on the hill. Your valley will be dedicated to the Holy Family."*

Then on May 23, 1988, she said, *"...My guidance will not lead you astray. I have the complete plan as to how this will all come together. Trust and do as I ask of you. You worry because you can not see the master plan of what will take place. Just have faith my children..."*

Finally a decision was made to write a letter to Mr. Gary Cusamano, Chief Executive Officer of Newhall Land and Farming Company; but there had been some disagreement in the group as to how the company should be approached. After all, business corporations weren't exactly accustomed to receiving letters stating the Mother of Jesus wanted a piece of their land. Nevertheless, a letter was sent. The communication was short and simple, definitely not a proper business proposal. The future would prove a lesson in hindsight.

The reply came and the company was not interested in making the land available for any purposes other than their own. What is interesting about the parcel is that because of the rocks and hills, it is not really suitable for any type of development, farming etc.; but it does appear to be a suitable site for a monument and shrine. Now it was evident that the only alternative was to follow Our Lady's message of daily meditation and prayer.

Prayer Group Core Leaders Step Down

The Feast of Pentecost, May 25, 1988, arrived and the resignation of the core leaders became effective. Their new apostolate and role as intercessors had begun. The Pastor's acceptance and notice to the prayer group members, associate pastors and parish council of St. Louis de Montfort expressed surprise.

> *...It is in the Spirit of profound thanksgiving that each of us has received the gifts of the Holy Spirit. Most especially we must give thanks for the gifts of love and service that have been continually present in our Parish Prayer. The Spirit never ceases to surprise us with the call to service. The members of the Core Group have long felt a second call, and the time has come to begin answering it more directly. In order to do this they feel it necessary to resign from their present positions...They will be working closely with me in allowing new leadership to come forth from within the prayer group.* [excepts of letter dated May 25, 1988 from G. Garcia, Pastor]

The prayer community was as surprised as the pastor, and many did not understand the leaders mysterious call; but in no time a new leadership emerged with a smooth transition. The old leaders continued to pray and assist Charlie and Carol in various ways, as Carol was still receiving the inner locutions from Our Lady.

On May 27, 1988, the Blessed Mother gave an encouraging message: "...*Take heart in my guidance. Do not worry as you tend to do. I will always be there. My children, each little change is part of my plan. All will go well. You are participating well in the challenge I am giving you...*"

A bold decision was then made to take Carol's messages to the priests in Medjugorje in June for discernment, before going to see Bishop Ziemann. On May 31, 1988, Carol was told by Our Lady: *"What you gain in your journey will help to transform my valley's plans. Do not worry about what you are to do. Just be ready to seek and bring forth what I ask of you..."* Anticipation mounted.

"The City of Peace"

A significant event happened before the pilgrimage to Medjugorje. On April 4, 1988, Our Lady had said to Carol, *"...Many will come and many will stay in my City of Peace."* The group had reflected on her words for some time; and motivated through prayer, they set out to confirm the Virgin's designation for her city of Santa Maria. If this is really what she wanted, it would be affirmed by the city government with an adoption of a formal resolution, they thought.

One of the leaders, a man named Pat Shelton, received the inspired words for the City of Peace resolution during his daily prayer time. It was prepared and scheduled for presentation to the Mayor and City Council the first week of June 1988.

The group arrived at the city council chamber with a few butterflies in their stomachs but also with a confident assurance that Our Lady would prompt the government leaders — after all, the city bears **_HER_** name and she **_is_** the Queen of Peace they thought. The full council made its stately entrance into the lofty chamber. With an echoed bang of his gavel, Mayor George S. Hobbs Jr. called the meeting to order. An animated pastor from one of the local churches touched everyone's heart as he voiced a lengthy opening prayer for Peace. After the opening prayer the city clerk was asked to read the resolution. This was it! Hearts pounded with expectation. Comments from each council member showed overwhelming support of the proposal. Then the vote was cast. It was a unanimous adoption of Resolution 88-50. So, on June 7, 1988, the city officially became Santa Maria, "The City of Peace." Had Our Lady softly whispered in the ears of government leaders once again? Was this another sign of her plans?

City of Santa Maria Santa Maria, California

RESOLUTION NO. 88-50

**A RESOLUTION OF THE CITY COUNCIL OF THE CITY OF SANTA MARIA
DESIGNATING SANTA MARIA AS THE CITY OF PEACE**

WHEREAS, we the community wish to thank our leaders for their unselfish and oftentimes unrewarded commitment to our city's growing needs; and

WHEREAS, the community acknowledges the policy of the city's leaders and government to provide a peaceful atmosphere in which we live, raise our families, work, and retire; and

WHEREAS, the city of Santa Maria promotes a spirit of pride in its growth, loyalty, charity, and brotherhood; and

WHEREAS, the city of Santa Maria aspires to the ideals of supportiveness, fairness, equality, honesty, and prosperity for all; and

WHEREAS, the city of Santa Maria provides a solace for all surrounding communities; and

WHEREAS, the city of Santa Maria, as the heart of the Central Coast, promotes growth with a sincere devotion and dedication to keeping the city safe and peaceful; and

WHEREAS, the community of the city of Santa Maria recognizes the need for a resolution which reflects the purpose of the city;

NOW THEREFORE BE IT RESOLVED that the City Council of the City of Santa Maria hereby designates the city of Santa Maria as

"THE CITY OF PEACE"

PASSED AND ADOPTED at a regular meeting of the City Council of the City of Santa Maria held June 7, 1988.

Mayor George S. Hobbs, Jr.

Mayor Pro Tem Thomas Urbanske

ATTEST:

Council Member James A. May

City Clerk Mary O'Brien

Council Member Curtis Tunnell

Council Member Robert S. Orach

Resolution 88-50

Chapter 5

Mid-Day

On June 8, 1988, Our Lady made plea for more prayer and gave a clear warning that Satan would be active, continually attempting to disrupt peace and interfere with her plans: **"My children, pray with me, so you may receive the graces I have for you. Be in harmony; do not let Satan make a division among you. Your prayers are important to bring this about..."**

Good News From Medjugorje

The trip to Medjugorje was enlightening. To think that Carol's messages had to be taken half way across the world for a preliminary discernment was mind boggling. The priests gave a positive opinion about the messages she had received to date (June 1988) with an assurance they did not conflict with Scripture, faith or morals and seemed consistent with Our Lady's call for Peace in a time when the world is swallowed by egoism, worldly pleasures, practical atheism and no need for God.

One of the first questions asked of Carol by a priest in Medjugorje was *"do you have a Spiritual Director."* Of course the answer was, *"no,"* because there had been a systematic refusal by the clergy in Santa Maria to become involved with such matters. The priest said that Carol would have to pray and ask Our Lady to arrange for a priest somewhere to guide her — even if that meant going out of town.

On return to the United States intense prayer ensued for a priest who would be open to giving Carol counsel and also in assisting the group.

The Door Opens

My husband and I had taken his elderly mother (who lived in Santa Barbara at the time) to Medjugorje. Shortly after our return she asked us to speak to her parish (San Roque Church in Santa Barbara) Rosary group about the trip and our experiences there. What started out to be a presentation to a small group was rapidly becoming a large group of many parish organizations. As a result we then insisted that we first confer with her pastor, Monsignor John Rohde, and receive his permission. That meeting took place in July of 1988. My husband and I and Charlie and Carol were then scheduled to give a talk about Medjugorje in August at his church parish hall. Much to our surprise over 300 people attended!

During that first meeting with Monsignor Rohde my husband and I had explained the dilemma Carol was confronted with regarding her messages to have a Cross built in Santa Maria and her need for guidance. He said he would be open to meeting with Carol and listen to her story. After several additional meetings he made a prayerful decision to give counsel to the group but only with the Regional Bishop's permission. Bishop Ziemann gave Monsignor Rohde his approval in the fall of 1988 with a subsequent confirmation given by Archbishop Roger Mahony.

Meeting with the Regional Bishop

When Charlie, Carol, my husband and I met with Bishop Ziemann, he listened carefully to Carol's account of the locutions from the Blessed Virgin. His advice was loving and pastoral. In the spirit of a true shepherd who directs with wisdom and prudence, he made several suggestions: wait and see if the locutions continue or stop; don't let anyone try to change the design of the Cross; and wait to see if there might be a request for a chapel. The reference to a chapel seemed to have a rather prophetic ring at the time and greatly surprised us.

He made it very clear that as a Regional Bishop he was taking a fundamental line of caution, neither saying Carol's messages were or were not from the Blessed Mother. **"That will involve a discernment process,"** he said. He expressed a personal opinion that regardless of whether Carol's messages would eventually be determined to be from Our Lady or from human inspiration, he supported the idea of building a Cross — it would be a good project. Knowing the land was in private ownership and in a different diocese than where Carol lives, he also made a profound statement: **"The real miracle will be the actual erection of the Cross."** He cautioned against diffusing the messages at the time and emphasized that Carol was not to be a focus. He also called for much discretion asking everyone to always be obedient to Monsignor Rohde.

Bishop Ziemann is a man with great insight: *"Everything may entail an immense struggle, trials and tribulations,"* he warned. *"If things are too easy, there will be no spiritual growth."*

A "Medjugorje Style"
Prayer Group Forms

During the next months many people wanted to know about our experiences in Medjugorje. The local newspaper had heard about our trip and wanted interviews. What was Our Lady saying to the young people there? Question after question after question.

Eventually we decided to give informative talks and share the Medjugorje messages from Our Lady Queen of Peace. Because we were not allowed to speak about Medjugorje in the parishes, a meeting room at a local bank was obtained. The people came and the gatherings increased to a point where a bigger facility was needed. Finally a large community room at Marian Residence, a retirement center in Santa Maria originally established for religious sisters, was obtained. A weekly Rosary prayer group was formed and patterned after those in Medjugorje.

The number of people continued to increase each week, oftentimes overflowing into the hallway. Everyone was hungry to know about the apparitions in Medjugorje and the Blessed Mother's call to the world. They came from surrounding communities and eventually from all over the state of California. The fruits were amazing with many conversions. People began to deepen their prayer life, return to the church and the sacrament of reconciliation. The non-Catholic people who came learned about Our Lady and gained an understanding of what it is to be a Catholic Christian.

Carol's Messages Stop

On September 2, 1988 Carol received her last message. It seemed to finalize all that she had received from the Holy Virgin since March 24, 1988. *"My children, the beauty on the hill will come as my children open their heart and the love flows from within."*

During the early days Carol's messages were not known to the public at large. Only a small number of people, a few priests, the Regional Bishop and Monsignor Rohde were fully aware of what was happening. Discretion was important during this time. In late 1988 the large prayer group was informed about Carol's messages from Our Lady, and everyone was excited about the request for the erection of a Cross overlooking the Santa Maria Valley.

Chapter 6

Late Afternoon

The Model of the Cross

Several men in the group had quietly started building a beautiful model of the future Cross in May of 1988. It is an inspired work of art and skillfully fashioned, each section fitted with precision. On the twenty-third of May Our Lady had even given a message to the men through Carol saying; *"...My Son is pleased with your design. The boldness, strength, beauty and grace are combined with the most important, love from your heart. It reaches out to all of my children..."* The model is made of polished stainless steel, wood and golden stained glass where the nail holes were. The completed project had taken many months to be built and was displayed for the first time at a private home in December of 1988. A small group of lay leaders in the community gathered for it's unveiling.

A public display of the Cross model eventually became a source of controversy and ultimately the first division among the original group. The builder-donors did not feel comfortable using the model to publicly promote the Cross as long as the Newhall Land and Farming Company adamantly refused to make the site available. The situation was a bewildering problem. In the best interests of everyone, the builder-donors consequently decided to suspend their active participation with the group. They had the four foot Cross blessed by a priest and have reserved it for the future when a site becomes available. They wanted it to be used to further a harmonious purpose. The final destination of the model was the Regional Bishop's residence where it remains to this day. Anyone who wishes to view it must pay the Regional Bishop a visit!

Plans to Publish the Messages

By January of 1989 plans were being finalized to release Carol's messages. A meeting with Bishop Ziemann was also held at this time to give him a progress report on the project and make him aware of some of the tensions in the leadership. Keeping his neutrality, he guided the meeting with his usual wisdom, asking the group to continually discern their real purpose and to always look for peaceful solutions. He seemed to know how difficult the project would be.

The Leadership Continues to Fracture

Over the next weeks everything moved at a swift pace causing a multitude of tensions, so much so, that in February of 1989, shortly before the release of Carol's messages, a second and more serious fracture of the leadership began to take place. An engineer who had joined the inner group thought the structural plans for the Cross could proceed immediately. He was also under the false impression he would be paid for his work in the very near future. It now seemed to the leaders that things were on the verge of getting out of control on a number of fronts.

Charlie was privately expressing his desire to quit his job and work full time on the Cross project. He wanted to form a nonprofit corporation that would be a vehicle for raising money for his ministry. The leaders involved regarded some of his ideas as going against the grain of the whole project and the intent of the Blessed Mother's messages to Carol. And, certainly no money could be solicited for the actual Cross because the land was not available. Charlie's promotional style, coming from his background as a salesman, was not agreeing with the mainstream of the leadership whose perception of implementing Our Lady's plan for the Cross embraced a total volunteer effort by everyone.

Keeping in mind the strict criteria the Church uses for judging the authenticity of private revelations intended for the public, the leaders were also concerned with how a possible Church Commission might view the project if Charlie and Carol were to receive any personal financial benefit. Even with the best of intentions, a potential source of scandal for Carol as well as the Church should be avoided.

Charlie kept insisting, and the disagreements continued. Finally, one of the leaders named Rick Bonanno, a psychologist by profession, called for a meeting with Monsignor Rohde to discuss the situation and attempt to resolve the conflicts. These were very distressing trials for Carol — a sticky situation. She was the very individual the leaders were trying to protect, and now she was caught between her husband's desires and a prudent check by the rest of the leadership.

On February 12, 1989, Monsignor Rohde moderated a heated meeting in his office for the better part of an afternoon. The leaders thought that their discernment and appeal for caution regarding the direction of the Cross project had value. They pleaded with Charlie to weigh their concerns. Eventually Monsignor Rohde asked Charlie if he understood the discernment and magnitude of what the other leaders were trying to express. His answer was "**no**." The Monsignor attempted to summarize and clarify what had been said but to no avail. Charlie was firmly set in his ideas and was not willing to accept the prudent view held by the others. The meeting ended in a spirit of mutual respect and tolerance for each person's convictions, but the leadership was shattered and the wounds cut deep.

Monsignor Rohde could see he would be called to the depth of his being as an instrument of Christ's Peace. All would require profound prayer and trust in the Lord, as the weather ahead might continue to be unpredictable days of radiant sunshine and torrential storms. Santa Maria would continue to be a difficult orchard to cultivate.

Some of the problems stemmed from the fact that Charlie had only lived in Santa Maria for about four years and had not experienced nor suffered the trials and tribulations of the early days in the prayer groups. He often expressed an opinion that the sufferings of the past were not relevant to the present. Had he forgotten so soon that the clergy in Santa Maria had not accepted Carol's messages from the beginning?

Other problems stemmed from a concern about agitating the land owners. However, the greatest apprehension of the leaders was that without continued discernment the foundation they had built for over a decade would go up in Satan's smoke splitting the community who was now beginning to support the project with enthusiasm. Only the future would prove if their insights had any value.

Some of the old leaders did not stop attending the Tuesday night prayer meetings at Marian Residence but attempted to be reconciled by maintaining a modest presence and a low profile. They also continued to welcome and pray with the pilgrims who came to the hill on the week-ends.

Carol's Messages are Released

A small booklet had been designed and sent to the printer with the title *"A Cross Will Be Built...,"* and distribution started on March 24, 1989. A young man in Santa Barbara generously provided funds (originally intended to pay for his trip to Medjugorje) for the booklet to be printed in Spanish as well.

As soon as the messages began to be disseminated, the number of people coming to the prayer meeting on Tuesday nights and to the hill during the day grew even larger. Pilgrims came to the hill especially on the weekends.

Then it happened! The foreman of the ranch received a directive from his supervisor: no one was to be allowed up on the hill. It was now off limits because the great number of people presented a liability to the land owners. For awhile there were some problems because the foreman would occasionally find people from out of town trying to sneak up on the hill at night. That resulted in no trespassing signs being posted on the property with warnings of prosecution. Everyone obeyed.

On the Roadside

During the next year and a half, people continued to gather and pray on highway 166 across from the hill on a right-of-way owned by the state of California. Initially these were small groups, but later large groups often numbering five hundred assembled.

News travels fast and it didn't take long before the media became aware of the events near the hill. Reporters hungry for a new scoop converged from many parts of the state, spoke with the pilgrims and then sent their stories over the wire service. The local television stations interviewed Charlie and Carol as well as the pilgrims. Information was now streaming across the United States and eventually across the world.

With all the publicity, Newhall Land and Farming Company soon found themselves in an even more precarious predicament. They continued to reaffirm their judicial position and became progressively more disturbed. The fact that the highway department had given permission for the people to gather on the side of the road and the California Highway Patrol was very cooperative in keeping the traffic flowing was a great source of irritation to them. Even though the people were not gathered on their land, they became so disturbed with the promotion of the project they fired off letters to state and county government agencies, then to some of the local priests, and finally to the bishops of each diocese (Monterey and Los Angeles) expressing their distress.

On a local level the clergy continued to try to suppress and discourage all of the activities and pilgrims by frequently saying they didn't know anything about the future project. Visitors from out of town who inquired at a parish office or rectory would often be told that the Church didn't support the project, and the pilgrims would be asked to not try to find Charlie and Carol or the hill. Some people were even told that the Noles were out of town on vacation, when in fact they were welcoming pilgrims at the hill.

Nevertheless, the people came. They were orderly, they prayed, they were healed, they converted, and they turned back to God. There was a "climate of faith" and the fruits were evident. The Christian people who live in Santa Maria and most especially the members of the various Catholic prayer groups in town welcomed the pilgrims, listened to the sorrows of their hearts, prayed for the sick, ministered to the needs of broken families and directed them to the Sacrament of Reconciliation and the Holy Eucharist at the local churches.

The atmosphere near the Cross site was definitely different. Passers-by would slow their speeding vehicles to look with awe at the mix of people praying near the busy two lane highway that serves as a main route between the San Joaquine Valley and the Pacific Coast. Most often, there would be a number of musicians in the crowd playing their guitars. The joyful music and enraptured singing would resound in the open air with an almost heavenly quality.

It is difficult to imagine this small oasis situated alongside a rural California highway. For someone who has never been to the site, what comes to the mind's eye at first glance is rather a mystifying picture: traffic zooming by, hundreds of people crowded on an embankment, no restaurants or sanitary facilities and a forbidden hill in the near distance. How could such a place be conducive to prayer? Would Our Lady really be at work extending her graces, blessings and favors on the side of a busy roadway?

For many people who had already been to Medjugorje, it was almost like being there all over again. For others, it was a first sojourn to a confined refuge of spiritual hope. Some came as curious skeptics; others with a firm faith. Why?

Grace was flowing in this rolling area of golden pasture land. It was an unusual, yet poignant scene of raw Christianity: people to people; black, brown, red, white and yellow; all seeking the heart of God through the Motherly intercession of the Blessed Virgin Mary. Some of the pilgrims received a special spiritual favor now and then, others saw signs and wonders in the sky; but there was nothing hysterical or fanatical taking place, just love in action among a diversified mass of humanity. Spiritually hungry, they yearned to be filled with "Peace beyond understanding."

As in Medjugorje, it was the people who made the difference. They were beginning to find the life of God in each other. There were no barriers between the people who came, just an obstacle with the land — it was not available.

Chapter 7

Another Time Zone

For the believers, Our Lady's apparent plan for the Central Coast of California and now a seemingly more specific plan for Santa Maria began to take on a new light. Between the summers of 1988 and 1989 many of the Catholic Christians began to sense a strong link between Santa Maria and Medjugorje.

Monsignor Rohde's Trip to Medjugorje

As Our Lady's call to the world continued to spread, more and more people from the Central Coast of California made a pilgrimage to Medjugorje. Monsignor Rohde made his first journey in July of 1989 serving as Chaplain for a pilgrimage my husband and I had organized (our second trip). Bishop Ziemann also traveled to Medjugorje in September.

While we were there, Monsignor Rohde spoke with Ivan Dragicevic, one of the Medjugorje visionaries, about the Cross project in Santa Maria. Our guide told us Ivan had already received the Cross messages which had been translated into Croatian for him. The conversation was video taped for viewing by the prayer group on our return to Santa Maria.

Msgr. Rohde:
Ivan, thank you for taking this time to be with us. Father Pavich talked once about the Holy Spirit and the Blessed Virgin working in all communities.

We believe that's happening in our community of Santa Maria, California. I'm not asking you to say that you believe it or don't believe it, or approve it. But, what I want to get out is that we know you went through a lot of difficulties. We go through a lot of difficulties with the hill where the Cross is supposed to be built. The people who own the land will not let us go on the property. We believe that Mary said we will have the land (eventually). I believe we should be obedient to what the owners say and I would like to have your comments about obedience.

Ivan:
To be obedient is very important in these modern times, especially when you look at obedience from the point of view of yourself as priest.

Msgr. Rohde:
She (The Virgin) said that there will be no barriers, but we seem to have these barriers.

Ivan:
Don't fight these barriers by force but just pray and try to win conversation with these people (the owners) to find a solution to your problems. So— pray and converse with these people.

Msgr. Rohde:
That's one thing that we've been trying to insist on — that we gather twice a week for the Rosary.

Ivan:
It's a good idea.

Msgr. Rohde:
We thank you and hope you will pray for our Cross project — to the Virgin for us.

Ivan:
Tonight at the apparition time I will recommend in my prayers to the Blessed Mother everything that we have said today; and if we pray together and really put all our thoughts together, I don't doubt that the fruits will come through our prayers.

Msgr. Rohde:
Thank you Ivan, for responding to <u>our</u> call.

Ivan:
You're welcome.

Our Lady Queen of Peace appeared to Ivan on Apparition Hill at ten o'clock in the evening while he was with his prayer group. The message she gave to him was a continued call for everyone to live the messages she had been giving since 1981. Ivan also told us that when she departed she went back to Heaven leaving the sign of the Cross in the sky that night.

Monsignor Rohde shared the video tape and our experiences of Medjugorje at the August prayer meeting. He encouraged the people to continue in prayer and asked for their obedience. He also said he felt he would ultimately be the one who would speak with the board of directors of Newhall Land and Farming Company, but that would only happen in God's own time.

Chapter 8

A Time for Change

A New Home for the Prayer Meeting

In the early fall of 1989, the crowd at the Tuesday night prayer meeting had grown so big that the number of people exceeded the fire safety code for Marian Residence. A gentleman named Charles Augustus, who later passed away, made arrangements with Fr. James Cadera, Pastor of St. Joseph's Catholic Church in Nipomo, California for the prayer group to meet in the church parish hall. This rural parish in the Monterey Diocese serves about 500 families and is located north of Highway 166 in San Luis Obispo County.

In one sense, the Los Angeles Archdiocese seemed to be "off the hook", at least for the time being, because all of the activities now centered in the Monterey Diocese, just on the other side of the Santa Maria River. Bishop Thaddeus Shubsda had become the heir to Archbishop Mahony's dilemma.

More Trials and Confusion

The Cross project is often like a roller coaster ride moving from a tremendous amount of fervor and zeal to frustration, discouragement and perplexity. Without a doubt the Blessed Virgin had foreseen the complexities of the project because she had encouraged everyone through her messages to have faith and not be impatient, but she had also said her plan would **"flow smoothly and quickly"** [May 23, 1988]. In human terms the erratic delays seemed contradictory because obtaining the land was now emerging as an insurmountable obstacle. The people had been praying and praying for over a year, and any negotiation with the Newhall Land and Farming Company was still a moot question. Their board of directors had become so antagonized by the publicity regarding the project that the doors appeared to be closed forever.

This dilemma began to cause uncertainty and confusion among the prayer group as a whole and especially for the people who live in Santa Maria. Those who voiced their distress and chagrin were often offended by Charlie's curt quips when they started to question the direction of the project. Many people thought his quotes of Carol's messages were beginning to sound like a fifth Gospel, and this became a bona fide concern.

Serious scrutiny is always part of the discernment process, and the large prayer community was now on the verge of a rupture. Answers were needed as tensions mounted.

There were other legitimate concerns as well. By early November of 1989, some of the people began to wonder how the future Cross could continue to be promulgated on a wide scale if the land was not available. At this interval it also became difficult for the people who regularly attended the prayer meeting to separate whether the primary purpose of the meeting (in addition to prayer) was for spreading Our Lady's messages and teachings of Medjugorje, for extensively promoting the project of the Cross, or both. This was an indigenous problem because at this time the majority of people who came on the week-ends to pray near the highway were out of town pilgrims. The group who came to the Tuesday night prayer meetings were primarily the people who lived in Santa Maria and the immediate vicinity.

After a few intense discussions with Charlie, more local people splintered off and formed small "Medjugorje Prayer Groups" in their homes, continuing to pray for Our Lady's intentions, her plan for the valley, and the eventual erection of the Cross. When the "natives" began to separate from the large group, Charlie would tell them, *"You're really not walking away from me and the Cross project; you're walking away from Our Lady!"* His comments caused people to feel guilty and more confused.

As a result of these frustrations a meeting with Monsignor Rohde was held. The outcome was a request for an additional meeting with Bishop Ziemann for "airing" their feelings and opinions. The meeting with Bishop Ziemann was scheduled to take place November 12, 1989, in Monsignor Rohde's office in Santa Barbara. It was supposed to be small, private and discrete (about 15 people including Charlie and Carol). Surprisingly at the last minute it took the form of a large assembly, 70 additional people having been invited by Charlie. The parish hall had to be used to accommodate everyone.

Bishop Ziemann Speaks to His Flock

Bishop Ziemann is not a man of pious platitudes but exhibits a unique style and charisma when relating with people. He is candidly sincere and has a great gift of teaching, but his most striking quality is his giving of self with a true sensitivity and receptiveness to each person. He explained his position and made sure his flock understood that he was not indifferent to them.

How do we know these locutions are true? The bishop doesn't know that the locutions are true at this point...I am not neutral to you and that's important. I am very close to you in prayer, supporting your growth in prayer. I have explicit confidence in your spiritual director guiding you in prayer. Basically what I'm trying to do as Regional Bishop is to be open to what's going on. It is a possible venture, only to the extent that it is created out of unity or causes unity. Unity, bringing people together in prayer and solidarity— that's Church!

He also made reference to the fruits reported to him.

That's what I've seen on the periphery because I haven't really been with your group at all. That's what I've heard from Charlie Nole, from Monsignor Rohde — and by the fruits you will know them. The fruits are the beauty of this Cross of Peace Project, whether the Cross is built or not. Whether or not it is built is in the design of God. I don't know His design...The church always takes a cautious view. The ones that are true are the ones that persist and are discerned — waiting, discerning, and praying. If it's the Lord's work, it will flourish; if not, it won't...

I'm a strong believer in the Blessed Mother, I pray the Rosary every day and know that she has appeared many times, in many ways, publicly and privately. I have no doubt about that. Whether this is one of those as far as the locutions go — I'm not saying she appeared visually-we'll just have to wait and see.

That's about where we are...If it's the Lord's work, it's going to flourish as long as we don't put obstacles in its way. If we put obstacles, it may still flourish, but many times, it doesn't because we can say I don't want that grace, the grace of devotion to Mary, and then we don't receive it because we refused it, so we have to be open...

If the Cross (project) becomes an idol, it becomes our God; it possesses us. The Lord doesn't want that. The Lord wants our wills; He wants our devotion especially through the Blessed Mother; He wants our prayers; He wants our dedication. If the Cross (project) is why you are together, it's what is bringing you together; it's a focus; it's a goal, but it's not an idol, not a God.

With or without the locutions, the building of the Cross may be a good idea. Supposing we're no further along in 1993 than now, then none of those prayers are wasted; we're all closer to the Lord; we're all saying, 'Thy will be done...

I certainly support all the work that Monsignor John Rohde has done... People not involved with you, who haven't prayed with you, it's hard for them to understand what's been happening...Invite people to pray whether they be lay people, religious or priests...

Stay with the faith you have received, stay with the Lord, be patient and pray, and know what is more important than even the Cross — and that is very important — is the building of community that is necessary before you build the Cross. The Cross becomes then, a symbol of the unity that is there. [Audio tape transcription]

The Bishop's words of wisdom had meaning for everyone present. It was a continued call for prayer, discernment and waiting — something the community had been doing for years before Carol ever received the messages to build the Cross overlooking the Santa Maria Valley. His words were a relief to those who had been made to feel guilty. His warning about obstacles and idols were a forthright teaching on how things can get out of control.

Would the Tuesday night prayer group continue to splinter, or would it become a cause for unity bringing people together? Would the priests in the area accept the invitation to come and pray, discern and wait with the people? Time would verify that it would not be easy.

The rifts are still taking time to heal and those who separated persevere in prayer. They have a solidarity behind the Cross and are in one accord for Our Lady's plans, but not everyone was ready to return to the group on Tuesday nights. It would take more than a band-aid to heal the pain. One might say, that after this extremely rocky period, an uncanny unity in diversity began to develop among the people in Santa Maria.

A Non-Catholic President

The organization for the Cross project continued to re-establish its leadership and brought a new group of assistants on board. Charlie said he now believed that he and Carol had been entrusted to carry out the project of building the Cross, and it now would be necessary for him to quit work so he could devote full time to establishing a non-profit corporation for the realization of their goals.

As the organization developed, with a small board of voting directors, Charlie assumed the office of vice-president and a gentleman named Don Davis became the president. He is a realtor with whom Charlie worked. He became interested in Medjugorje and the Cross for Santa Maria when Carol was receiving her messages.

Mr. Davis is not a Catholic and his new position on the board puzzled the Catholic community. Why would a non Catholic assume the office of president? Ultimately Charlie explained to the prayer group that he had interpreted the Cross project to be an ecumenical project and not solely a Catholic project.

Mr. Davis is a poised public speaker with a very congenial personality. Because of other obligations, he rarely came to the Tuesday night prayer meetings; but when anything official happened, he would come and speak to the assembly. It was difficult for him to field questions regarding Catholic matters, and he would frequently have to say he was not knowledgeable about the practice of the Catholic faith or the norms of the Church. Since the priests in Santa Maria did not attend the Tuesday night prayer meetings, nor did Fr. Cadera, Pastor of St. Joseph's, the people would sometimes have to await a periodic visit and counsel from Monsignor Rohde who lived 65 miles away.

The absence of a priest on a weekly basis was an unfortunate burden for the Tuesday night prayer group to bear. Even though Bishop Ziemann had encouraged the group (at the November 12, 1989 meeting) to invite the local priests to come and pray with them, the invitation was seldom accepted. To this day there has never been a **team** of Santa Maria priests or deacons to assist Monsignor Rohde on a weekly basis with pastoral care of the pilgrims or the activities of the Cross of Peace movement.

Many of the people in this predominately Catholic prayer group continued to quietly question the new composition of the board with a non-Catholic president. It was an odd turn of events because the prayer group practices Catholic devotions, and in recent years the Sacrament of the Eucharist had become the focal point of the Anniversary Celebrations of Carol's messages. They also questioned why an ecumenical project ministry with a non-Catholic president would then place itself under obedience to the Catholic Church, especially when the president did not fully understand the faith and was not required to be obedient to Church Authority.

Medjugorje has perhaps had the greatest trials and conflicts of any supernatural phenomena in the history of the Catholic Church (now including a civil war in the country). The dimensions of ecumenism surfaced there also; but the villagers were fortunate to have the local Franciscans involved from the beginning, and theologians eventually clarified the issues. The community in Scottsdale, Arizona also had the advantage of the local clergy guiding the people from the beginning, when the locutions and apparitions began occurring there. Sadly, Santa Maria has never had the same benefit.

For the pilgrims who proceeded to stream in from out of town the internal conflicts were not widely known, and the various prayer groups continued their fervent prayer always welcoming those who came on pilgrimage. The graces from Our Lady were still flowing abundantly despite all the local turmoil and strife.

Chapter 9

Half Past Four

The Madonna is Here!

The community was jolted beyond belief when on March 24, 1990, The Feast of the Annunciation and the second anniversary of the Cross Messages, Barbara Matthias a pilgrim from Southern California reported to Charlie that the Blessed Virgin had appeared to her at the hill and given her a message.

Barbara had made a previous pilgrimage to the future Cross site earlier in the month with a group of her friends but did not receive any special favors from the Holy Virgin on her first visit.

After telling Charlie about the apparition she gave him the message which she had written on a *Cross Will Be Built...* booklet. Charlie, in turn, notified Monsignor Rohde. Barbara returned on the following Wednesday March 28, 1990, and Our Lady appeared to her again giving another message. Charlie tried to keep everything quiet but the news was leaking out rapidly. Then at his request Barbara quit her job in Southern California and moved to Santa Maria on March 31, 1990, to live with Charlie and Carol.

On April 3, 1990, Charlie astounded everyone present at the Tuesday night prayer meeting with an amazing report. He made an announcement that Fr. Cadera had told some of his parishioners after Mass on Sunday April 1, 1990, that the Blessed Mother was rumored to be appearing at the hill; and Fr. Cadera believed it. He then declared to the large crowd (which was video taped by several people) that everything was true. He commented further by saying that the messages Barbara was receiving were more important than the "Cross of Peace" messages. He gave "tid bits" of information indicating the Blessed Mother's messages would probably be printed and released by Easter Sunday April 8, 1990.

After so many years of expectant faith and anticipation that something big might eventually happen, the Madonna herself had come — not to a couple of children from a Catholic grade school nor to a religious sister in a convent, but to a pilgrim from out of town. What a bombshell!

The roller coaster was moving uphill again, and the word was spreading like wildfire. During the next few days the people in the prayer group experienced a myriad of emotions — perplexity and electrified excitement.

At first no one really understood exactly what was happening and the rumors were rampant. When Charlie brought Barbara to the hill around four in the afternoon, he secluded her near his car that was parked in a special place, away from the crowd, and would not allow anyone to go near her. Several men surrounded the vehicle acting as security guards threatening people with citizen's arrest if anyone crossed a certain line. My husband and I, unaware of the restrictions, were personally threatened by one of the men who also informed us he had earned a black belt in Karate. We politely suggested that he realize he had no such jurisdiction and his behavior wasn't very Christian, but retreated to keep the peace. He had an intimidating assurance of his role as guardian and was definitely a person with whom my husband did not want to become entangled.

As the days progressed, Charlie finally made a decision on April 14, 1990, to allow Barbara to kneel for the apparition on the bluff beside the roadway. She was now part of the crowd but was immediately whisked away as soon as the apparition ended. This was for the purpose of recording the message which Barbara was required to start writing as soon as she got in his car to be driven home.

Our Lady's messages were not disseminated to the public at Easter time by order of Bishop Ziemann and Monsignor Rohde. They both agreed that a discernment process should take place. But Charlie was enthusiastic and zealously continued to give little hints to the people. Sometimes he would indirectly reveal a few lines of the messages to the pilgrims on the highway and then further captivate everyone's curiosity at the Tuesday night prayer meeting. He candidly disclosed that the messages were so beautiful he would be moved to tears every time he transferred Barbara's hand written account to his computer. These comments caused everyone to eagerly await the messages with an inquisitive expectation, but an unusual enigma seemed to veil all that was happening.

Before Barbara's state of ecstasy lengthened to more than three hours, she would join the Tuesday night prayer meetings after Our Lady had departed. She was 43 years old at the time and remained very discrete, rarely saying much at all. She helped Carol sell religious items at the book table but was not allowed to discuss the apparitions nor the messages with anyone. Consequently no one knew much about Barbara.

After a certain period of establishing a protocol for the apparitions at the hill, the people began to deepen their prayer life and became resigned to waiting patiently for the messages to be released. The one thing they did know was that the Blessed Mother was appearing to Barbara under the title "Our Lady of the Immaculate Heart"; that fact had leaked out over the past several weeks.

Signs and Wonders

The signs and wonders increased and so did the length of the time of the apparition. In the early period Barbara's state of ecstasy gradually progressed to nearly six hours. During the week people came to the bluff on the highway in the evening, praying and singing much like Ivan's prayer group who gathers on Apparition Hill in Medjugorje. On the weekends thousands of pilgrims would arrive throughout the day awaiting the 4:30 P. M. appearance of Our Lady and then remain praying the Rosary late into the night.

Incredible phenomena were observed: the "Miracle of the Sun" during the day, luminary signs at night, Rosary links and medals turning gold in color, extraordinary photos, cures and conversions. One night forty people all claimed to see the Holy Virgin depart to Heaven.

Although this account is not meant to give all of the many details surrounding the time when Barbara was receiving the Blessed Mother at the hill, I want to mention the children. Time and time again children would give witness to extraordinary signs. A common testimony was their observance of seeing everything enveloped in a golden cloud including cars on the highway, birds, airplanes and the people in prayer! The children came with their parents from near and far. At first, I thought they were probably experiencing a form of collective illusion, but the incidents occurred on different days with different numbers of children whose ages generally ranged from four to twelve. Some would see and some would not. I finally came to a conclusion there was no collective hallucination; however, I did not understand what the children were talking about until I had the same experience. For me, the grace only happened once — on Sunday afternoon April 15, 1990. During the apparition I was sitting and praying on the bluff across from the hill when I saw a large black crow soaring in the sky. Every time it flew over the hill it would appear to be enveloped in a small, brilliant gold cloud. When it flew away from the hill, it looked like a typical black crow and no cloud remained. Since I am very objective about these things, I thought I was suffering from a hallucination of some type myself. But I knew better after watching and double checking with people sitting next to me (who saw the bird but not its gold color). The day was warm and clear with not a cloud in the sky. It sounds rather strange and I have no explanation. However, I then knew what all the children were witnessing, and I believe them. I later heard the testimony of several adults who saw the same thing happen when a small aircraft flew near the site — they said it turned gold only while flying over the hill. Some people would "see"; others would not. It seems that this phenomenon may be peculiar to Santa Maria as I have not heard of anything similar happening at other apparition sites.

An impressive testimony which I have on video tape is the account of an eleven year old boy named George who knelt next to Barbara during the apparition of Tuesday April 24, 1990. He saw Our Lady and described how she looked and what she was wearing that day, but he said the Virgin did not speak to him. Later in evening he gave his testimony to about 300 people gathered for the prayer meeting at St. Joseph's in Nipomo.

A week later I mentioned the apparitions at the hill to a priest in Santa Maria whom I thought might now be open to the happenings. He said to me, "What's so special about Our Lady possibly appearing in Santa Maria?" I was surprised by his question and answered with a question of my own. *What if she has a message for the people?* I asked. "How could she have anything different to say than what our bishops tell us?" he responded. I replied by saying, *"Our Lady is now appearing in many places of the world, and people are turning back to her Son because of her special presence and the graces she is pouring forth at the apparition sites. How many lives are the bishops touching with their words and presence at this dark time in history? Maybe she is needed now more than ever."* He pondered my statements and questions further, but gave me no answer — only a puzzled look.

In Santa Maria, a reoccurring "Cross of Grief" seems to frequently overshadow a future "Cross of Peace", but Christ and the Blessed Virgin would tell us the two go together: The Cross of Golgotha included great suffering as well as hope, grace and peace. This also appears to be true of most authentic apparition sites. Fatima, Lourdes and La Salette are prime examples of suffering, trials and favor in the approved apparitions. Medjugorje which awaits judgement by the Church is the foremost case of a modern day apparition site that endures profound suffering and grace. Only through agony, pain and spiritual affliction does it seem that Santa Maria may have its day of "resurrection" and unification as well.

Chapter 10

Hours of Confusion

Monsignor Rohde's Difficult Role

Guiding a visionary is not an easy job for a Spiritual Director. St. Theresa of Avila and St. John of the Cross mention in their writings how difficult it is for anyone who is receiving spiritual experiences to find a director who is both learned and familiar with the mystical life — especially that which is undefinable. I have asked many priests about their seminary training in mystical theology, and they have all told me it is extremely shallow or non-existent. Order priests have more training than diocesan priests, and those living in monastic communities often have the most experience. Contemplative religious sisters are frequently well qualified, and lay ministers who have completed training courses for spiritual directors can also be very competent. By in large, those best qualified exercise a charism for spiritual direction that is given by God.

Barbara was unable to obtain a priest Spiritual Director in Santa Maria as none would accept. Ultimately this burden, almost by default, fell on Monsignor Rohde who was guiding the "Cross of Peace" movement at the time. Since he is also the pastor of a parish 65 miles away, it was impossible for him to direct Barbara on a weekly basis. He is the first to admit this was a difficult task. But he is open to the

Holy Spirit and has a special love of Our Lady, so he accepted the role with the intention of doing his very best.

Charlie also tried to zealously give guidance to Barbara on a daily basis; but he did not have a background in spirituality, discernment or theology. She was not allowed to work or visit with friends, and her life was quickly beginning to lose autonomy. Unfortunately she was also required to write about everything she experienced during the ecstasies which eventually augmented the record to be inclusive of private conversations with the Blessed Mother, commentaries relating to her personal life, private questions and answers, and descriptions of the visions she experienced during the ecstasy. When the ecstasy progressed to six hours the account became an arduous process. Attempting to be as precise as possible, Barbara would sometimes stay up until three or four in the morning journaling the messages. Consequently this resulted in confusion, needless proliferation, and mixing the private messages with the public messages. Eventually, with the help of her spiritual director, lay ministers, theologians and priests schooled in mysticism, the private and public messages were later discerned and classified into separate journals.

In May of 1990, the "Cross of Peace" organization launched a fund raising campaign to generate money for supporting Charlie, Carol and Barbara entirely from ministry funds, and to provide finances for administrative needs and traffic safety on the roadway. Don Davis, President of the "Cross of Peace Corporation", published a special announcement with the appeal:

Two exciting milestones have just been reached by the Cross of Peace Ministry. First, we prayerfully announce that Charlie and Carol Nole and Barbara Matthias are now devoting their full energies in support of the Cross of Peace. This tremendous walk in faith is supported by the heartfelt conviction that Our Blessed Mother wants their 100% efforts in support of Her Project.

This is a milestone in the "Cross of Peace'" Ministry. It now means that Charlie and Carol who were the first to be touched by the Blessed Mother over two years ago, and Barbara, who is receiving blessings from Mary daily are now devoting their total time to the activities surrounding the "Cross of Peace". It also means that they must derive their own support entirely from the ministry...

The announcement also spoke about the record crowds at the hill and a request from the highway department to control the parking of cars and safety of the pilgrims.

...We are looking into measures such as a temporary concrete barrier and shuttle buses to move people from the site to a safer parking area...

Although having a full-time ministry and providing for traffic safety are exciting events, they are also costly. The ministry has never needed to run a funds campaign, but these situations now make such a campaign a necessity.

We are asking all who support the Cross of Peace to consider both a one-time donation for the specific purpose of highway safety/access and an on-going monthly pledge to support the ministry itself. Any amount you can give would be very appreciated...

...Also please understand that this invitation to participate in the Cross of Peace Ministry does not in any way intend to siphon funds which you have committed to your own local church.

*Mary has asked all who can, to come and partici-
pate in the building of her Holy People and in the
Cross. Those are our goals with this Ministry. May God
bless you for your support.*

*Don Davis, President
Cross of Peace* [Notice of 5-8-90]

But on Friday May 11, 1990, Barbara received a
message from our Lady saying,

*...My Children I am very concerned about the idea
of you raising monetary funds for the undertakings of
the Cross of ... project. Consider that this could turn
people away from the project and away from Jesus and
me. Trust that this money you want to raise will be
taken care of by voluntary donation — by persons who
just give freely without your raising funds...*

This message was one of many that caused a disas-
trous conflict between Barbara and Charlie. Since the
messages had not been released, the public was not
aware of the frictions taking place in the Nole's home.
But unknown to Barbara, the community was already
reacting against the solicitation of funds and the Regional Bishop's office was being contacted. Within a
few days he put a stop to the campaign, requiring any
pledge money received to be returned to the donors.
On Monday May 14, 1990, further discord erupted
when Monsignor Rohde failed to communicate directly with Barbara a request he wanted her to make of
the Blessed Mother. He was attempting to discern the
length of her state of ecstasy and transmitted an appeal through Charlie asking Barbara to request the
Virgin to end the apparition at sundown that day.
Barbara did not want to honor the request believing

she could not tell Our Lady what to do. Extremely upset, she attempted to contact Monsignor Rohde by phone, but he was not available and could not be reached by his secretary since he had already left for a three day meeting in Los Angeles. Barbara was in tears and everything was in an immense state of confusion. A heartbreaking argument took place between Barbara and Charlie, who was now accusing her of being disobedient to the Monsignor.

Ultimately the strife between Barbara and the Noles reached a point of no return. They did not understand her state of ecstasy or her handicaps and finally concluded she must not be authentic. A number of distressing disputes continued; and as a result, Barbara became so distraught that she made a comment that "maybe the Blessed Mother will just come and take me home, and all the turmoil will be over." Charlie apparently misconstrued her comment as a suicide threat and proceeded to make an alarming phone call to her brother in Escondido asking him to rescue his sister from this allegedly sad state of affairs. Charlie consulted with Monsignor Rohde, and then made a decision to remove Barbara from his home. The problems were more than he and Carol could handle. It had now become necessary to separate the visionary from the locutionist, with the idea of relocating Barbara back to Woodland Hills as soon as possible.

Barbara was requested to pack up her belongings and immediately move from the Nole's to the apartment of two young ladies who had pledged their assistance. The girls had agreed to drive Barbara, on the coming week-end, to her niece's home in Woodland Hills, for counseling by her brother.

So in the course of seven days, the appeal for monthly pledges intended to provide Charlie, Carol and Barbara with living expenses, as well as administrative costs for the ministry was halted by Church authority; the benevolent relationship that Charlie, Carol and the "Cross of Peace" officers had established with Barbara was decimated; and Monsignor Rohde had become totally confounded by all of the latest disharmony. Would there ever be peace in Santa Maria? He did not know what or whom to believe. Satan had driven another wedge, only this time it appeared to be a stronghold.

In view of the fact that neither the prayer group nor the general public had any knowledge of these tribulations, much of what was happening behind the scenes was not disclosed.

Chapter 11

Hours of Grave Trial

When the morning came for Barbara to be driven to Woodland Hills, the girls whisked her off to ten o'clock Mass before leaving town, and then drove her to the hill. Barbara had no idea that this little side trip had been planned as her farewell jaunt to the future Cross site. Nor did she have any idea that all of her things had been stashed in the trunk of the car. The hidden agenda seemed to constitute the banishment of Barbara from Santa Maria forever because she had now become a hindrance to all of the "happenings" here.

Then they headed out of town, but Barbara asked them to exit the freeway and return her to Santa Maria: they refused. She asked again, telling them she had decided not to go to Woodland Hills; but they wouldn't comply. Then a third time, she pleaded with them to take the next exit and return to Santa Maria. Once more they refused by reminding Barbara that she was suicidal, and they had an edict to get her to her brother as soon as possible. Barbara continued to plead with the girls but to no avail: they were not about to change their minds. Barbara cried and argued with them for a number of miles but finally gave up, deciding to explain everything to her brother when she saw him.

Her trials in Woodland Hills included heated, tearful, discussions with her family, and eventually a visit by the police, who had been called to take her to a mental health unit for a 72 hour "hold" and psychiatric evaluation. Barbara's family does not practice their Catholic faith, and they thought she might be anxiously overwrought, rather than suicidal. They did not understand how she could be seeing an apparition of the Blessed Mother and thought maybe she should be examined to see if she might even be a "little crazy". When the police arrived, they just laughed and told her brother it wasn't their job to get involved in apparitions. "Seeing the Blessed Mother wasn't a crime nor a reason to detain anyone," they said. As far as taking her to a mental health unit because she was suicidal, they could find no such "death wish" on Barbara's part, as she did nothing but speak about the beauty of life. Satisfied that she was not a danger to herself or society, the officers bid her a good evening and carried on with their law enforcement duties.

Later that night, Barbara finally agreed to go to a clinic for an evaluation to **prove** to her family she was not suicidal or "crazy". That was exactly what the intake professionals ascertained. They sent her home in a few hours with feelings of great compassion for all that had happened to her over the past week.

The two girls came the following morning to see if Barbara had been admitted to a hospital but were amazed to find her at her niece's house. Barbara thought they would take her back to Santa Maria; however, they unpacked her belongings from the trunk of their car and decided to leave without her. Barbara remained with her family for several days to recover from her exhausting trials; and after she felt rested, her brother then drove her back to Santa Maria.

When I later spoke with her brother, he told me he was shocked when he received the telephone call from

Charlie stating Barbara was suicidal. But he was concerned about his sister and wanted to help her if anything was really wrong. He also said that Barbara had always been very religious, and nothing made any sense to him — especially suicide. He did not want Barbara to return to Santa Maria because he could not understand why she would even desire to return to a place where she was not welcome. He said he only complied because Barbara had told him that the Blessed Mother wanted her to remain in Santa Maria.

A Retraction

On May 22, 1990, the Cross of Peace Corporation published another surprise announcement entitled, *Where Do We Go From Here?*, which retracted the organization's proposal of two weeks prior.

> *Faced with choices every day, we all pray for the wisdom to select the right path to follow. If we find we have chosen wrong, we hope to be able to find our way back to the starting point and to try again. The Cross of Peace Project has been through this very process these past two weeks.*
>
> *Some of you may have received a letter describing a fund raising campaign which we felt was necessary at the time. After prayerful consideration, we have decided to return to the beginning and rescind that request and the pledge campaign. Any funds which were sent to us in response to that letter will be returned to you.*
>
> *The reasons for this action are many. They include a firm adherence to the Cross of Peace messages that the "funds will be bountiful..." and that many will come and participate as they are able to in this effort...*

Therefore, we feel it is important to be true to the spirit and intent of the original Messages of the Cross of Peace. We are not, then, soliciting pledges. However, we do invite all those who wish to help with their time, talents or in any other way to contact us. As we mentioned in our recent newsletter, "We are not asking for monetary donations to support the building of the cross...However, we are accepting contributions for our current and on-going ministry..." [*Cross of Peace*, Public Notice May 22, 1990]

People really had no idea what was taking place but information gradually filtered out that the Cross of Peace organization was having some internal problems. Once again it was a time of much confusion and suffering.

Monsignor Rohde's Statements

Subsequently, Monsignor Rohde issued a statement to the prayer group relating concerns regarding Barbara. On May 29, 1990, the bombshell was dropped. Although the statement never mentioned Barbara's name, it said, "There was a serious doubt concerning the alleged apparitions and messages that had been taking place during the past couple of months... There were questionable facts and statements contained in the messages which the Spiritual Director did not accept...There were serious questions about the stability of the visionary who did not want to follow the advice of the Spiritual Director, and therefore, he could not accept the alleged apparitions or the messages." The statement also mentioned that the Spiritual Director had met with Bishop Shubsda in Monterey who was in the process of setting up a commission to investigate the entire Cross of Peace Project.

Everyone at the prayer meeting was speechless because two months earlier they had heard Charlie say he was moved to tears by the beauty of Our Lady's messages to Barbara. What had happened? At the time, a complete explanation was never given, which left the people in a state of shocking bewilderment. Had she just disappeared from Santa Maria? No one really knew.

Barbara Is Publicly Scandalized

After returning to Santa Maria, Charlie let Barbara know, in no uncertain terms, that she was not welcome at the Cross of Peace Prayer meeting; neither did he want her to come to the hill nor attend the Saturday evening Rosary at St. Mary's Church. Desiring to disassociate her from the Cross of Peace movement, he persecuted her with sharp words and Monsignor Rohde's statement against her. On June 2, 1990, Barbara and a friend attempted to peacefully join the group of people praying alongside the highway. As Barbara approached the place of prayer, a confrontation with Charlie took place. He threatened to read Monsignor Rohde's negative statement to all the pilgrims and point her out as being psychologically unstable. Since Charlie didn't want anything or anyone to destroy the Cross of Peace project, his emotions were tense and fearful, and his reactions were far from being cool and collected. Barbara's life was now being made as miserable as possible, but she accepted her crosses interiorly as well as exteriorly.

Monsignor Rohde had not expected the statement to be used inappropriately, nor was it his intent to forbid Barbara from praying the Rosary with the group in the Church or at any other place for that matter. Fortunately for Barbara, he intervened by putting a stop to this impulsive and indiscriminate use of the statement. From that time on Barbara received the apparition each day privately.

For awhile, Barbara stayed with an elderly lady who lived a short distance from the Church, but finally she ended up in a deplorable boarding hotel where life with the riffraff of Santa Maria would eventually become almost intolerable. The new situation Barbara found herself in was a far cry from the secure environment of the religious cloister she had known less than a year ago. She secured a part time job to pay for the rent and sustained herself on very little food; frequently eating nothing more than canned food for supper, as she didn't have cooking privileges at the hotel.

Several weeks after the people had been stunned by the negative announcement about Barbara, someone in the crowd at the Tuesday night prayer meeting, was brave enough to ask the "sixty-four thousand dollar question": "What really happened to the visionary Barbara Matthias?" A gentleman from Santa Maria, who was on the platform at the end of the meeting, casually leaned towards the microphone and informed the hundred plus gathering of people that Barbara was no longer associated with the group, "and, besides that, she is schizophrenic," he said. Oh, how pitiful, everyone thought privately. Not another word was said!

A Reflection on My Emotional Reaction

I had not been an avid supporter of Barbara. In fact, I had only met her once; and our conversation was nothing more than a hello, I'm pleased to know you. But, as I listened to his nonchalant explanation, my entire being was consumed with outrage. How could this man make such a public statement about her without any medical proof. I thought about standing up and reproving him; but I was so angry and so completely dumbfounded, I couldn't even speak. I didn't know if I was experiencing justified anger or sinful anger, and all I could think of was no human being should have to go through this type of public slander in a Christian community. If this is what love is all about, I must be in the wrong place, I thought. And, to observe that his statements had been taped by several people with video cameras was more than I could handle emotionally. I wondered just how far this calumny would go.

From that moment on, I was resigned to pray for Barbara and love her in some mysterious way through Our Lady. I did not return to the prayer group on a weekly basis; and neither did many others, because at this point, the roller coaster had gone down hill nearly smashing the community to shreds. However, I did continue to go out to the hill and pray with the pilgrims until the end of June 1990 when the gatherings were no longer permitted. From that time on, everyone was required to meet on the grounds of St. Joseph's Church in Nipomo.

What was happening in our beautiful "City of Peace?" I silently retreated to my interior life with the Lord and Our Lady, trying to grasp an insight. For several months all kinds of thoughts raced through my mind: What would the Bishop or a Commission think? How would Monsignor Rohde handle all the problems? Was the local clergy right in staying out of the Cross of Peace activities, or was it because of their absence that everything was out of control? Why was the Lord allowing this terrible disunity to prevail? Would there ever be an answer or a peaceful solution to this entangled mess? I also reflected on Our Lady's words to the present visionaries throughout the world: *"Wherever I come, Satan comes also."* Had I, someone who should know better, also forgotten that Lucifer wanted to destroy the Holy Virgin's plans for the Valley — and for peace? The problems in Santa Maria had become extremely complex,m and the powers of darkness now appeared to be at work in an astounding way, I concluded.

Sometime later, I found out that other people were as upset as I had been that night, but they had also remained silent. They could not comprehend why, either. It was seemingly part of a mystery which could not be fully understood. I sought the advice of my spiritual director, who asked me to continue to pray and wait on the Lord and the Blessed Mother. *"Eventually you will have your answers,"* he said.

My husband and I escorted a third pilgrimage to Medjugorje in early July of 1990. While I was there, I regained my inner peace; but I still wondered when Our Lady's plans for Santa Maria would move foreword in tranquility. The answer as always, was "Pray, Pray, Pray".

Chapter 12

Dinner Time

My First Meeting with Barbara

In the latter part of September 1990 I was asked to meet Barbara. Some of her friends had planned to have dinner with her, and they wanted me to come and listen to her speak about the appearances of the Blessed Virgin. I thought it was odd that I had been invited, but I was interested. I was neither a believer nor an unbeliever in her apparitions, but I felt compassion for Barbara, and I had an open-mind. It would be an opportunity to discern for myself. After all, I had been praying for her since May; and on second thought, this might be a divine appointment arranged by Our Lady — how did I know?

On October 2, 1990, I visited with Barbara for the first time across a cheerful dinner table simply set with a floral patterned table cloth. We enjoyed ourselves over a delicious home-made dinner.It was a warm friendly atmosphere, and Barbara's expressive hazel eyes and ear to ear smile reached out to everyone who had gathered to share the meal.

Barbara was born with Turner's Syndrome, a sex-linked chromosomal defect that affects 1 in 2,000 women. Instead of the normal 46,XX complement, about half of the women with Turner's Syndrome are missing an X chromosome, which gives them a 45,X pattern. It is characterized by short stature, sterility and a variety of secondary physical defects which may be present both externally and internally. With the exception of the short stature, the secondary symptoms are varied in their degree of severity — from hardly noticeable to very apparent. Despite Dr. Turner (who is now deceased) being careful to point out that these patients have normal verbal intelligence, those who are untrained observers with limited knowledge, often make the faulty assumption that Turner's women are mentally retarded. Turner's patients have good general intelligence but most have lower performance IQ scores. The performance problems appear most distinctly in unstructured tasks that require spatial or distance judgments, and certain hand-eye motor coordinations (such as driving a car with gear shifts). Mathematical calculations, especially geometry, present a classic difficulty for women with Turner's Syndrome. They can learn these tasks, but at slower rate than others. These women have a high capacity to deal with stress but often have immature social skills which may affect their ability to form close friendships. [Jana L. Orton, *Health and Social Work*, May 1990, pps. 100-105.]

Some of the characteristics related to Turner's Syndrome are strikingly evident when one first meets Barbara. When she relaxes or listens intently to someone who is speaking, her eyelids and facial muscles tend to droop somewhat making it easy to misread her expressions. Others, such as her minor heart defect, are obviously not apparent.

Barbara, now age 46, is very petite in stature (4'8") and full of animated energy. Her short brown hair frames her fair-skinned face, which almost seems to glow with a radiant countenance when she describes the Blessed Mother.

Barbara wears glasses and hearing aids in each ear, as her hearing impairment is moderately severe. It was apparent to me that when several people are engaged in conversation at the same time, she can have a difficult time discriminating their speech patterns; but for the most part she compensates fairly well when the ambient noise level decreases.

Her childlike simplicity and bubbly joy are unmistakable when she speaks. She frequently uses expressive hand gestures while talking which gave me the impression she might be Italian. I later found out that she has a Portuguese lineage, although she was born in Brazil. Barbara converses very intelligently; but due to her handicaps, she has a tendency to interrupt or be repetitive when trying to make a point or be understood. These traits could cause Barbara to be misinterpreted by some people as being a little self-centered, but as you get to know her you realize these characteristics are part of her handicap.

I immediately perceived that she is very unpretentious and has an unsuspecting, innocent naivety when it comes to cosmopolitan activities. In fact it was my conviction that her rather nonplused perception of certain social situations could make her very vulnerable to being mistreated or even exploited in a variety of circumstances, especially if the situation was trying or precarious.

Her simple and rather uncoordinated attire is notable and indicates her austere material poverty. She told me that blue is her favorite color because blue is associated with the Blessed Mother.

Difficult Rows to Hoe

Barbara had two tragic marriages between 1967 and 1980 and then pursued a religious vocation in New York in 1983. However, her handicaps proved to be an impediment to becoming a nun, and she was therefore deterred by the convent council from taking final vows in 1989. When she returned to California, she came to Woodland Hills and stayed with her niece. Adjusting back to the secular environment was a big transition from her religious vocation — especially after having been in a cloister for nearly five years. Her life has still remained one of temporal poverty.

She Touches the Mother of God

When Barbara gave me her testimony about the daily apparitions of Our Lady, she related a very rational account of how she sees her, hears her, and touches her. She also described some of her visions while in the state of ecstasy and how the Blessed Mother appears to her most of the time.

She comes on a cloud, in a brilliant white light: a light like nothing on earth. Usually she is dressed in all white with gold trim on her mantel and a gold belt around her waist. Her hair is chestnut brown; she has rosy cheeks and a delicate mouth. Her eyes are a beautiful penetrating blue; in fact, they melt you in her love. Her voice is the most gentle loving voice I have ever heard — it is very difficult for me to explain.

On special occasions or special feast days she is dressed differently. On the Feast of her Queenship she is crowned with 12 golden stars and wears a jeweled gown. Most of the time she comes with the Infant Jesus and angels, but sometimes other saints come with her too.

In the course of the five hours I spent with Barbara and her friends, never did I observe the personality of a schizophrenic. Having worked in the field of special education for many years, what I did observe was a very misunderstood, handicapped woman whose virtue, humility and spiritual life would put most of us to shame. From my experience as a lay minister I had no reason to believe she was lying about the apparitions, nor did I believe she was under the influence of demonic spirits. If I had any particular criticism of Barbara, after learning about her life, I might say that she tends to be a little too scrupulous.

Before leaving that evening, I asked Barbara if I could have a copy of her messages from the Blessed Mother. Since they belonged to her, she said she had no problem allowing me to read them; but she had given them all to Monsignor Rohde. She suggested that I call him and ask him to send them to me. Several days later I called him, and he verified with Barbara my permission to read all of the messages. I never spoke with Barbara again until June of 1991.

Chapter 13

A Time for Discerning

For the next eight months I poured over the daily messages and came to the conclusion that something had to be done. It was easy to spot the subjective elements, private information (not the secrets) and awkward syntax; but, I thought they were important, and most of all I could see that "Our Lady of the Immaculate Heart" was speaking to Her Children through Barbara. And, besides that, Our Lady had asked many times in the messages that they be released. If nothing else happened, I felt compelled to at least have Barbara's human dignity as a person restored. I didn't even know if that would be possible after all the damage that had been done.

How to proceed? That was a question I wasn't quite sure about, so I just prayed for the whole eight months - Dear Lord, and all of Heaven, if you want these messages released and Barbara's dignity restored, please send the right people to get the job done.

During these eight months I would hear horrible rumors around town about Barbara: "Poor thing she's just having hallucinations; she's a clairvoyant; she's probably oppressed by the devil; she must be mentally ill." The rumors went on and on and on, but I remained silent.

My Prayers Answered

In summer of 1991, my prayer was answered. A nurse practitioner and hearing specialist from the San Francisco Bay area, named Anna Marie Maagdenberg, had seen Barbara as a patient. She had also been present during the apparitions while Barbara had been visiting there. In the second week of June, she came to Santa Maria to make an adjustment on Barbara's new hearing aids. It was through a rather "divine orchestration" of Our Lady that I came to meet her on the weekend she arrived in town. After a lengthy discussion, we concluded there was enough positive evidence to warrant a serious inquiry into the apparitions Barbara was receiving.

The Bishop Dies: Decisions Made

The Most Rev. Thaddeus Shubsda, Bishop of Monterey Diocese, had died of cancer in January, and it was difficult to ascertain the status of the Monterey Commission that had been established to investigate Carol Nole and the Cross of Peace messages and activities. Barbara had not been part of the Commission's probe so it was hoped that an autonomous inquiry would finally dispel the rumors and answer the questions that so many people had raised over the past year. Since the faithful are permitted to request a competent examination of extraordinary phenomenon, a decision was made to initiate an independent investigation of Barbara by qualified experts.

Mrs. Maagdenberg is a generous, compassionate, self-giving Catholic Christian, who has a sharp discerning mind and proficient medical expertise in her field. We contacted Monsignor Rohde and received his blessing to proceed. He, in turn, informed Bishop Ziemann.

Answer the Question, Once and for All

Now, the questions would be answered once and for all. If Barbara was mentally ill, get her proper treatment; if she was possessed, get her an exorcist; if she was neither, examine the phenomenon, scrutinize the messages, and evaluate the fruits.

It was agreed that the independent investigative team would use the criteria set by the Church for formal investigative procedures and the scientific-medical model would initially follow the one used in Medjugorje. Priests and theologians would be brought on board to assist in the discernment process, and Monsignor Rohde would participate with them. But it was also agreed that nothing would commence until Barbara's permission, and the permission of the Blessed Mother, was obtained.

The last week in June 1991, Barbara asked Our Lady for permission; and it was granted. Barbara welcomed the investigation and was willing to cooperate in the discernment process and the demanding scientific studies which would require a number of months to complete.

Serious Scrutiny Begins

In late July of 1991, the great Marian theologian, Fr. Rene Laurentin, an expert on Lourdes and Medjugorje, came to Santa Maria to meet with Carol Nole and the people who had experienced graces and conversions associated with the Cross of Peace movement. Prior to Fr. Laurentin's arrival, Charlie had asked Monsignor Rohde if he thought Fr. Laurentin should speak with Barbara. Monsignor Rohde said, "Yes, definitely."

Fr. Laurentin "Kidnapped?"

Because of the friction between Charlie and Barbara, Monsignor Rohde had made prior arrangements for Fr. Laurentin to interview her privately. The meeting took place in the late evening after he and Monsignor Rohde attended a potluck dinner with the Cross of Peace organization. Monsignor Rohde and Fr. Laurentin left the group around nine o'clock and did not return to Fr. Laurentin's hotel until after midnight. By the next morning that discrete meeting had become an unusual cross for both Fr. Laurentin and Monsignor Rohde. It eventually ruptured Fr. Laurentin's friendship with his escorts. The Monsignor was accused of "kidnapping" Fr. Laurentin who had freely chosen to visit privately with Barbara. For months afterward neither priest could convince the antagonists that Fr. Laurentin was entitled to make a free choice in his agreement with Monsignor Rohde. At this time Fr. Laurentin was given a copy of Barbara's messages for discernment.

Prayer Group Evicted

There were other trials as well. Two weeks before Fr. Laurentin's visit to the Cross of Peace activities, the prayer group had been booted out of St. Joseph's parish by the pastor. Fr. Cadera publicly expressed his agitation with the organization saying he had become increasingly bothered by the promotion of the Cross of Peace. He told everyone he had made his decision to evict the prayer group after consultation with the Monterey Diocese. Giving people an impression the Church was in favor of the Cross of Peace was something he had concluded was not appropriate, and he went on to publish his opinion in the church bulletin. He was also concerned that the Noles were drawing salaries for their efforts and spoke openly with reporters from several newspapers about his objections. When reporters asked him why he had allowed the group to meet at the church in the first place, Fr. Cadera said it was because he wanted to give them a place to pray. The group was obedient in leaving St. Joseph's Church grounds and finally ended up renting an office in Santa Maria, near the Ramada Inn. Charlie and Carol greeted pilgrims in their new book store and Cross of Peace Information Center or at the city park on the north side of town. The activities had now shifted back to the Los Angeles Diocese like a ping pong ball; and the ball was in Cardinal Mahony's and Bishop Ziemann's court once again.

In August of 1991, theologian Dr. Mark Miravalle of The Franciscan University in Steubenville, Ohio questioned Barbara at St. Catherine's Church in Burlingame, California. He received all of her messages and began his discernment. It was a smooth interview with none of the unfortunate problems encountered by Fr. Laurentin.

Chapter 14

Hours of Freedom and Change

At Dr. Miravalle's request, Barbara was removed from the despicable hotel where she was living and taken into the home of John and Barbara Gayton for the next six months. Conditions at the boarding hotel were unbearable. It became infested with cockroaches which Barbara said would crawl over her face at night waking her from her sleep. And Barbara's health was suffering also, as she had very little to eat. Her employer had reduced her work schedule from five hours per day to two hours per week because of her handicap, which almost eliminated her income. She was on the verge of becoming homeless once again until the Department of Employment had her hours restored.

A Scorched Spiritual Orchard

In early September, internal problems caused still another fracture in the Cross of Peace organization. More than twenty active committee workers had presented serious concerns to Monsignor Rohde relative to the Cross of Peace board about finances and the manner in which the members of the board had conducted themselves. Monsignor Rohde called a meeting of the two groups to resolve the difficulties. On September 11, 1991, prior to the meeting and subsequent to Fr. Laurentin's visit, he received a fax from President Don Davis informing him that the organization had selected a new priest to fill the role as Spiritual Director. Bishop Ziemann had also been receiving complaints from the committee workers regarding the management of the ministry. A meeting was held with the Bishop. The two sides were unable to resolve their differences, and one more time dedicated local Christians resigned with deep wounds. The spiritual orchard that Monsignor Rohde had tried so hard to cultivate in Santa Maria had been scorched by the flames of Satan one more time. Despite the continued trials and tribulations the community continued to pray for peace; and in the absence of Monsignor Rohde, Bishop Ziemann attempted to keep the organization on the right path.

Chapter 15

Scientific Twilight Zone

Over the course of the next several months a scientific team was established at the University of California, San Francisco Medical Center (UCSF) for the purpose of testing Barbara's state of ecstasy and her psychological equilibrium. The study began in October of 1991 and was completed in September of 1992. Monsignor Rohde, Anna Marie Maagdenberg and I participated in the study and observed the testing. Final tests were done in September of 1992 by Paris neurologist, Dr. Philippe Loron; UCLA physician, Dr. Antoine Mansour; and Fr. Laurentin. Interestingly, the religious background of the scientific investigators included: four Catholics, one Lutheran, one Quaker, one Buddhist, one Jew, and two agnostics.

The UCSF team was under the direction of William D. Hooker, Ph.D. and Linda Davenport, Ph.D., both neuropsychologists on the faculty of the Department of Psychiatry at the University of California, San Francisco Medical Center.

The qualifications of the experts are beyond reproach; and many of the professors are world renown for their expertise in their given fields, most having won many national and international awards for contributions to the various disciplines they represent:

Sumary Curricula Vitae

Felix Conte, M.D.
Endocrinologist and expert in Turner's Syndrome;
Professor of Pediatrics, UCSF

Linda Davenport, Ph. D.
Clinical Psychological Assistant to
William D. Hooker Ph. D.;
Assistant Clinical Professor, Division of Behavioral
Pediatrics, UCSF; private practice

Paul Ekman Ph. D.
Clinical Neuropsychologist;
Professor, Department of Psychiatry, UCSF;
Director, Human Interaction Laboratory and
world expert in nonverbal expressions of emotions
and facial mapping, UCSF School of Medicine

William D. Hooker, Ph. D.
Clinical Neuropsychologist;
Assistant Clinical Professor of
Psychiatry, UCSF; private practice

Robert Levinson, Ph. D.
Clinical Psychologist with specialty in psychophysi-
ology of emotion;
Professor of Clinical Psychology, UC Berkeley;
Director, Clinical Training Program and Psychology
Clinic, UC Berkeley

Jonathan, Mueller, M. D.
Neuropsychiatrist (Board certified in both neurol-
ogy and psychiatry);
Associate Professor of Psychiatry, UCSF; Director
of San Francisco Neuropsychiatric Associates; private practice

Charles Yingling, Ph. D.
Clinical Psychophysiologist;
Professor of Medical Psychology, Department of
Neurological Surgery, UCSF;
Director, Cognitive Neuroscience
Laboratory UCSF;
Director, Neural Monitoring Service, UCSF

Other examiners included:

Anna Marie Maagdenberg, RN, MSN, NP
Board Certified Nurse Practitioner/Hearing Specialist; Center for Hearing, Pinole, Ca

Philippe Loron, M. D., Paris, France
Neurologist;
Ancien Chief de Clinique a la Faculte, Praticien
Hospitaller a la Salpetriere;
Medical investigator, Medjugorje
Medical investigator, Shroud of Turin;
Medical investigator of oils exuding from Damascus
visionary; Medical investigator of oils and tears ex-
uding from statues and icons

Scientific Team Prepares for Study of Barbara

Monsignor Rohde made it clear to the scientific
team that from a Catholic theological point of view the
independent investigation had been initiated with a
hypothesis that the ecstasy and apparitions Barbara
was experiencing were theist and transcendent. With
this in mind the scientists were asked to **rule out**
hysteria, hallucinations, catalepsy, epilepsy, sleep and
dream states, self hypnosis or auto suggestion, schizophrenia, psychosis, neurosis multiple personality,
schizophrenia or any other pathological or psychological disease or disorder.

At Monsignor Rohde's request the team was very sensitive to the religious character of the apparitions and did not allow Barbara to be treated like a "guinea pig". Barbara had also agreed in writing that if her state of ecstasy could be attributed to natural or pathological causes, she would welcome their assistance and suggestions for a recommended course of treatment or therapy.

A month prior to the testing, key members of the team were given the scientific and medical reports of the Medjugorje visionaries to assist them in developing their model. At this point the reader must clearly understand that **the scientific testing of a visionary does not constitute an *objective* proof of the apparition;** this is beyond the realm of science. The scientific study can only assist in establishing what the visionary and ecstasy **IS NOT.**

Dr. Linda Davenport and Anna Marie Maagdenberg submitted preliminary summary reports to Monsignor Rohde, respectively on December 4, and January 11, 1991. Copies were also sent to Fr. Laurentin and Dr. Miravalle.

Monsignor Rohde's Conclusion

After receiving a summary report Monsignor Rohde communicated this letter to Fr. Laurentin:

February 10, 1992

Dear Fr. Laurentin,

On May 29, 1990 the Cross of Peace Corporation, released a statement I made regarding the reported appa-

ritions taking place in central California. I did not release the name of the visionary in my statement.

The reported apparitions have occurred in both the Diocese of Monterey and the Archdiocese of Los Angeles. The visionary resides in the city of Santa Maria, which is part of the Archdiocese of Los Angeles. The city of Santa Maria is situated on the border of each diocese. At that time, I was the Spiritual Director for the Cross of Peace Corporation.

I stated that there were questionable facts and statements contained in the messages, which I did not accept at that time.

I also stated that there were serious questions about the stability of the visionary and that the visionary did not want to follow the advice of the spiritual director and therefore I could not accept the alleged apparitions or the messages.

Since that time, the visionary Barbara Matthias has, with the permission of her spiritual director, willingly cooperated in an extensive evaluation of her spiritual experiences and state of ecstasy.

PURPOSE OF THE EVALUATION:

1. Rule out "faking" or "pretending" of the apparitions
2. Rule out organic etiology of the apparitions
3. Rule out psychological causes
4. Investigate cognitive processing as it relates to the experience

This evaluation included psychiatric examinations; psychological examinations; neuropsychological examinations; neurological examinations; audiometric examinations, including electronystagmography (ENG);

electrophysical examinations including electroencephalograms (EEG) and measurements of the autonomic and somatic nervous systems; facial mapping; magnetic resonance imaging of the brain; physical examinations; extensive interviews with Ms. Matthias and others. A review of the messages has also been conducted.

These examinations were carried out by teams of experts at the University of California San Francisco, Medical Center; The University of California Berkeley, Psychological Laboratory; The Center for Hearing, Pinole, Ca.; and in the private offices of the neuropsychiatrist and the neuropsychologist, San Francisco, Ca. Their curriculum vitae is available upon request. A preliminary report has been submitted for independent theological review.

Questions regarding the stability of the visionary have been resolved. In May of 1990 Barbara Matthias was not settled into a permanent living environment. She did not have employment or her own transportation. She has a severe hearing loss. All of these factors caused a lack of autonomy in her life at that time.

I made a statement that she did not want to follow the advice of the spiritual director. This involved a situation of faulty communication. I had transmitted a request to Barbara through another individual. This was a mistake on my part. Barbara refused to obey the request because it did not come directly from me. I have now resolved this issue. Barbara was justified in her refusal. The messages in question, received during a particular ecstasy, have been resolved to my satisfaction. The messages in question were not public messages. Barbara continues to follow the advice of her spiritual director and is obedient to Church authority.

I made a statement that I had met with Bishop Shubsda who was in the process of setting up a commission to investigate the entire Cross of Peace Project. Bishop Shubsda, of the Monterey Diocese, subsequently died in January of 1991. I do not know the status of a commission regarding the Cross of Peace Project. Barbara Matthias is not the subject of a formal Church commission.

As the phenomenon of apparitions is considered, I am reminded of your statement "that it is better to err on the side of caution than on the side of enthusiasm".

Jesus Christ has revealed all that is necessary for our Salvation. The purpose of an apparition is to recall the Gospel message, to bring the Gospel to life and to give hope. The body of Christ is charged with "testing the spirits" and holding on to what is good.

Within the confines of spiritual freedom as it relates to Christian life, we must not remain passive. The authorities and the faithful must respond to grace and co-operate in the discernment process.

I am satisfied with the sincerity of Barbara Matthias.

I am satisfied that her state of ecstasy has been verified by medical science. Based on the medical and psychiatric evaluations, I am satisfied that she is not "faking" or "pretending" the experience; that she is not psychotic; and that no organic etiology accounts for her experience.

Barbara Matthias is under the pastoral care of the Church through her spiritual director. The independent investigation by qualified experts is ongoing at this time. Final judgement always rests with Church authority.

Sincerely in Christ,
Reverend Monsignor John W. Rohde

All Elements Examined

Another part of the discernment process is the theological investigation which includes an examination of both positive and negative criteria relative to the visionary and surrounding events. Theologians discern the apparition as precisely as possible, and the process can often take a number of years. Qualified Church experts also examine whether the apparitions are in accord with faith and morals, Scripture and the Tradition of the Church; or are they a fake and a fraud. The diabolical must also be ruled out. And finally the fruits are scrutinized: are there conversions, healings etc. In Barbara's case, all of these elements were examined for nearly three years. The scientific testing was more comprehensive than Medjugorje and has surpassed that of any visionary tested internationally to date. The fruits will continue to be evaluated.

Quest of the Adversaries

Except for the inquisition initiated by her adversaries, Barbara's life began to become somewhat more autonomous. At the end of February, 1992, she and a friend secured a small apartment across from St. Mary's church where she presently lives. Since the apparitions were no longer public (as of May of 1990), Our Lady appeared to her discretely, every day, in the Church. But eventually the pastor forbade her from receiving the appriation of Our Lady in the church. Barbara was obedient, and since that time she continues to receive the daily apparition at 4:30 P. M. privately.

During this time her adversaries were busy trying to save the Catholic Church from Barbara, convinced it would be devastated if they didn't stop her crazy, frivolous apparitions. They spent months delving into her past marriage and divorce records, questioning people from California to New York, including religious sisters at the convents where she had been a "temporary professed". This was a difficult period for Barbara, but the Blessed Mother sustained her with special graces during each trial.

The Discernments of Fr. Laurentin and Dr. Mark Miravalle

In May of 1992 Fr. Laurentin met with the UCSF scientists in San Francisco and personally received their final report. His discernment and positive conclusion about Barbara, as well as Dr. Mark Miravalle's, are detailed in Fr. Laurentin's book, *The Way of the Cross in Santa Maria Part II: Beyond the Wisdom of the Wise* (1993, Queenship Publishing Co). He has stated in his book:

> *Barbara's ecstasies are spontaneous and not pretended. The clinical tests and observations, achieved with more sophisticated scientific equipment than at Medjugorje or Kibeho, (20 curves for the electroencephalogram) reveal a very profound ecstasy. Even the cerebral cortex is partially disconnected. (This is not the case with Medjugorje where the ecstasy is less profound.) Barbara's state of ecstasy is coherent and functional. It conditions her contact with the apparition. Her ecstasy is not pathological. She presents rather, a functional nature, according to the measure in which the disconnection with the ambient world condi-*

tions a coherent contact with the other world that she witnesses...It is an interpersonal and immediate communication which seems to reach the visual and auditory centers of perception...

Her sincerity and her coherence testify for authenticity of Barbara's spiritual communications, taking into consideration the relativities of such a discernment. In brief, for Barbara as for the other visionaries, the apparitions are not the beatific vision but a limited communication, which engages filtered and adapted in various degrees by the receptivity, participation, activity, and interpretation... Witness also in her favor her limpidity, and her naivety in the positive sense of the word. a total oblivion of self. stripped of all ostentation. she is relaxed, welcoming, kind and warm toward her interviewers. She answers only their questions without putting herself in front; without rambling; without talking to herself — a true abandonment to God in all circumstances, good or bad. She has therefore, an authentic supernatural life and this fact bears witness to the authenticity of her ecstatic communication within the control of the relativities stated...Certainly, the discernment must continue. It will progress but the ecstasy (well tested) and Barbara's edifying life permits the conclusion: "Blessed are the Poor". This conclusion converges with the opinion of Dr. Mark Miravalle, STD, theology professor at the Franciscan University of Steubenville, Ohio...[Rene Laurentin, The Way of the Cross of Peace in Santa Maria, 1993.]

Monsignor Rhode Revises His Opinion

July 20, 1992

To those present at the August 22, 1992 Public Meeting

Re: Barbara Matthias

In August of 1991, I had an extensive interview with Barbara Matthias at the parish site of St. Catherine's Catholic Church in Burlingame, California.

After this interview with Barbara and in terms of how her answers and experiences compared with other authentic apparitions of the Blessed Virgin in the rich history of the Church, I came to a firm theological and personal conclusion that Barbara was experiencing something authentically supernatural.

When I later examined the messages transmitted by Barbara, I found that there was a need for further discernment and clarification in distinguishing from the written text what was exclusively the message from the Blessed Virgin, and what was more in the category of Barbara's reflections and commentary also contained therein (almost as in a diary format).

*It was for this reason that I advised against an immediate publication and promulgation of the messages, until such time that a proper process of distinction and clarification could be made regarding the written text. **But to be sure, my advice against the immediate publication of the body of the messages should in no way be construed in any sense as a negative reflection on the supernatural reality of Barbara's experiences, for to discern precisely "what is from Mary" and "what is from Barbara" presupposes in itself the true supernatural presence of the Mother of God.***

Recent medical-scientific testing experienced by Barbara (possibly the most extensive for any reported vi-

sionary internationally to date) and its positive conclusions in favor of Barbara's psychological balance and her communication with the external world, add empirical confirmation that Barbara is receiving consistent apparitions from the Mother of Jesus.

Some have seen Barbara's special needs in regards to her Turner's Syndrome conditions as a remote difficulty towards her role as recipient of apparitions. I would disagree with such a hypothesis since the Turner's Syndrome, according to the input of the researchers, does not directly nor intrinsically impede Barbara's fundamental ability to transmit messages from the Blessed Virgin. Rather, the reality of Barbara's handicap seems to me to lodge Barbara in the category of the "blessed poor and little ones of God," who because of an honesty, humility, and innocence that can come through the purification resulting from exceptional crosses, makes them all the more suitable instruments for the transmission of messages from heaven.

In Jesus and Mary,
Mark Miravalle, S.T.D.
Associate Professor of Theology and Mariology
Franciscan University of Steubenville
[Letter of July 20, 1992.]

Chapter16

The Hour for "Bringing Believers Together"

On the Feast of the Queenship of Mary, August 22, 1992, Monsignor Rohde moderated a public meeting for "Bringing Believers Together" at St. Joseph High School in Santa Maria. Well over 400 people attended. The scientific report on Barbara was presented to the community by Anna Marie Maagdenberg, NP, who had conducted some of the scientific tests. Monsignor Rohde presented the church criteria for the discernment process, and I presented Barbara's life history. For those who were present the meeting cleared up the rumors about Barbara's state of mind and her daily apparitions of the Blessed Virgin Mary; Barbara was determined to be sincere and coherent; she was not faking or pretending; the ecstasy was not pathological.

Because the discernment process is so important, yet so confusing to many people, I felt it worthwhile to publish Monsignor Rohde's speech of August 22, 1992, in this volume, hoping the reader may grasp a better understanding of how the Church discerns. For ease of reading, indented italics are not used. The entire speech begins and ends in quotes.

How Does the Church Discern Religious Phenomena?

"First let us define who and what is the Church.

The Church is the mystical body of Christ — The People of God. The Church emphasizes that the People of God will assemble together and function together. The People of God as defined by Vatican II include the lay people, the religious, the clergy, the bishops and our Holy Father who is the Vicar of Christ. The People of God are to strive for unity in Christ even though they are diversified. God the Holy Spirit has gifts to give each person for the building up of the Body of Christ. His gifts are diverse but it is the same Spirit who desires to manifest Himself through the members of the Body. The Holy Spirit is always the binding force of unity.

Fr. Rene Laurentin tells us that, 'a judgement on the "signs of the times" has never been a monopoly of Church authority. The magisterium is the guide and the authorized guarantee. The Church **is not** a place where the "Light" would be the exclusive property of some, where others would only obey blindly. The Vatican II Council spoke reactively against this false and dangerous idea.' He goes on to say, 'even the successors of the Apostles are not exempt from any risks of human weakness; history proves it.'

Obedience to established Authority, and to the good order of the Church, does not necessarily extinguish an interior conviction nor the responsibility to prepare discretely a historical revision. Thus, it was for Joan of Arc, condemned and burned in 1431, through a matter of decision of a tribunal of the Church, constituted by the bishop of the place...Condemned by legitimate local authority of the local Church, Joan of Arc was later canonized by the Supreme Authority of the Church in 1920.' Father Laurentin wants all people to know that, 'the people are generally the first to believe in apparitions, and to know about them...Most often the laity has the pilot role...If their judgment is good, the authority will confirm it. If the people go astray it will rectify it after mature reflection.' He tells us further, 'If apparitions were the exclusive matter of authority, neither Guadalupe, Lourdes, Fatima nor other apparitions would have been recognized. They would have died without an echo. The Church would have lost, undoubtedly. She has recognized them because she was alerted by popular movement.'

He also says, 'It is normal that the impetus from the people anticipates the Authority. But, they must be prudent and respectful of the magisterium, who is endowed with a more decisive charism, in order to denounce the errors regarding faith or morals. The fifth Latern Council, which established legislation on such matters, INVITES BISHOPS TO SURROUND THEMSELVES WITH QUALIFIED EXPERTS in order to pass judgments. Experts are no longer forbidden to gather information and knowledge in an orderly manner in order to facilitate the judgement of the Christian people, and of the Authority itself, so that no one may go astray. One can easily go astray in many ways, through illuminism or rationalism, or credulity or criticism. An expert can provide service to the people and to the Authority, if he or she informs and judges **beyond** the passions and tensions which surround these affairs.'

It is to this effect that Fr. Laurentin increased his works and documentation, and called out a medical team of a very high level for Medjugorje. He says, 'the scientific work has eliminated a good number of untruths which come from excessive fervor or very often from opponents...A notable and sometimes major portion of my work consists of dispelling the anticipated errors of naive fervor and tense oppositions, which can be permanent sources of false information. After that, begins the real discernment process...

'As always, there are certainly some ambiguities, objections and difficulties...The transmission of heavenly communications is never one of absolute reliability...

'When the Church teaches revelation (faith and morals), she teaches it with authority. She requires absolute obedience... The assurance of the Church is something else when she judges the authenticity of an apparition — a fleeting historical event, a different fact of life in the Church. Is the Virgin appearing or is she not appearing? In attempting to answer this question the Authority of the Church **is not transmitting the word of God, it is revelation.** She expresses only the difficult and conjectural judgement.

'For the authority of the Church to recognize apparitions, Pope Pius X teaches in his encyclical *Pascendi*, "She does not wait to express her opinion on the **reality** of apparitions; she simply confirms that nothing in the facts which have been analyzed is in opposition to faith or morals." She thus gives a **Nihil Obstat** — a permission to believe...If a Christian has a reason to doubt that Our Lady appeared in Lourdes, he or she would not be in error...while to deny the Incarnation of Christ or other revealed dogmas is a mortal sin, which the Authority of the Church condemns with assurance and firmness.

'The freedom which the Church allows believers in the case of recognized apparitions, **also exists** in the case of apparitions which are not recognized. He who has good reasons to believe in them, like all of the pilgrims at Lourdes and Fatima prior to official recognition by the Church, does not sin and is correct in following his conscience — the Light of God in his or her life. And, it is a fact, that these "Lights" of the faithful ordinarily **anticipate** the judgment of authority... Everything orients itself in this sense: Accept and cultivate the fruits!...'

Scientific Study Results Revealed to Public

For the past two years, Barbara Matthias has been undergoing an independent study of her religious experiences, which include the transmission of heavenly communications and apparitions of the Blessed Virgin Mary who is often accompanied by her Son Jesus and/or other Saints. Barbara is under the guidance of the Church by her present spiritual director who is a Roman Catholic priest. I was formerly Barbara's spiritual director but have not served in this capacity since July of 1990.

The first stage of this process was conducted with much difficulty, in much confusion and with many mistakes being made.

The second stage has been in correcting misunderstandings, errors and false information; evaluating innocent zeal and tense objections; dispelling untruths regarding her state of ecstasy (which have included extensive interviews, medical and psychiatric evaluations by qualified experts; confidential tests to rule out diabolical apparitions; scrutiny of the messages by a group of theologians, priests, religious sisters and lay people). There is also a process of documenting the fruits.

Only one of Barbara's messages has been published and revealed to the general public. It is the message of September 10, 1991, printed on the invitation to this public meeting. Contrary to what some people may believe, Barbara's state of ecstasy does not last for six hours. This was the case from March of 1990, until late August of 1990. Beginning in August of 1990, the length of time gradually decreased. By December of 1990, the length of time in ecstasy had decreased to one hour and one half to two hours, and continues in this time frame at present.

Because of mistakes made with Barbara and others during the early stages, much confusion occurred.

Many people know that in May of 1990, I issued a negative statement about Barbara's spiritual experiences. In the early days, when her ecstasies lasted for long periods of time, she received many messages. Not living in Santa Maria, I was unable to guide her spiritually on a frequent basis. I also made the mistake of transmitting a request by telephone to Barbara through another person. Confusion resulted and Barbara refused to obey this request because she had not received it directly from me. I would like to state publicly, that Barbara was justified in not complying at that time. I had never guided a visionary before and have learned much from this mistake. With the help of theologians and members of the independent scientific team, I have now come to understand how messages from a heavenly source are transmitted through visionaries.

On February twenty-first of this year, I issued a new public statement which was based on the independent investigation of Barbara. The statement concluded with my personal opinion that I had no reason to believe that Barbara was not seeing the Blessed Virgin Mary. There were rumors at the time, that the statement was a forgery. To clear up the confusion, I would also like to state publicly that I **did** write the new statement which was also conveyed to Fr. Laurentin prior to its public issue.

There is also another matter which needs to be cleared up at this time.

In Fr. Laurentin's newly revised issue of the book, The Apparitions of the Blessed Virgin Mary Today, published by Veritas in Dublin, Ireland, a paragraph about Barbara Matthias reads as follows: *'The arrival on the scene of a certain Barbara Matthias, who pretended to be a visionary and was rejected by Monsignor Rohde, has somewhat complicated the issue. Nonetheless, there are many supporters who have had cures and other graces.'*

After this text was published, Fr. Laurentin was questioned about the statement and its source. In a fax dated March 6, 1992, Fr. Laurentin responded as follows and I quote: *'It seems that the word "pretending" is a very negative word in English. It is a mistranslation. My French text does not have this meaning or faint simulation. I wrote only '...Barbara Matthias who is also said to see the Virgin...' The word "pretend" does not translate my thinking. But, I would prefer to give my conclusions in a more positive and enlightening context soon.'* He also sent me a copy of the book, which I have here this evening, and he has also retracted the word *"pretended"* in his own handwriting as a footnote."

At the end of the program Monsignor Rohde read letters addressed to the community from Fr. Laurentin and Dr. Miravalle regarding their discernment and sincerity of Barbara. The final part of the meeting was for the purpose of reconciliation and forgiveness, and Monsignor Rohde ministered to everyone through a forgiveness prayer for spiritual and emotional healing. In closing, he reminded everyone that Our Lady is the Queen of Peace; and finally he exhorted the group to implore her intercession in having peace of heart restored to all of those who are working so hard to see her plans realized.

The people who attended listened intently to all of the informative presentations, and the meeting for "Bringing Believers Together" ended on a peaceful note. Everyone also thought it was an important step toward unity in the Santa Maria Valley. Several priests from surrounding communities attended, as did one Santa Maria priest and a deacon.

Monsignor Rohde Appointed Episcopal Vicar

On September 1, 1992, Monsignor Rohde was appointed by Cardinal Mahony as the new Episcopal Vicar of the Santa Barbara Pastoral Region to fill the vacancy of Regional Bishop G. Patrick Ziemann, who had recently been appointed Bishop of the Santa Rosa Diocese. Monsignor Rohde's new position now placed him back into the capacity of overseeing Santa Maria, but this time, on an elevated Episcopal rank.

Monsignor Rohde is to be commended for the extremely difficult role he agreed to assume. By assisting the people of Santa Maria and being open to Mary's Plan, he has surely been blessed with extraordinary graces from The Mother of God. The experience he gained will no doubt benefit him in guiding his flock — especially when it comes to discernment. The greatest gift he has given to everyone who lives here is his love for the Church and its people, his priesthood, and Our Lady. Our Lord is sustaining him as he continues to walk on the waters of faith, trusting and following in Peter's footsteps, as a man of great courage. No doubt the Lord will do great and wonderful things through him in the future.

Fr. Laurentin Returns to Santa Maria

Fr. Laurentin's third visit to the Central Coast of California took place the first week of September, 1992, in Santa Maria. On this investigative trip, Paris neurologist Dr. Philippe Loron and Mrs. Anna Marie Maagdenberg, NP, accompanied him. Dr. Antoine Mansour, a physician at UCLA Medical center in Los Angles, was also present for Barbara's apparition on September 2, 1992, in my home. He assisted Dr. Loron and Mrs. Maagdenberg in performing some of the final tests.

A Continued Struggle for Unity

Later in the evening, Monsignor Rohde moderated another unity meeting, only this time it was for a limited number of leaders in the various prayer groups of the community. Barbara was present, as were Charlie and Carol Nole. Don Davis, President of the Cross of Peace Corporation did not attend. Fr. Laurentin, Dr. Loron, Dr. Mansour and Mrs. Maagdenberg also joined the group.

The gathering was friendly; and a number of issues relative to Barbara, Santa Maria and the Cross project were discussed.

During the evening an interesting option was discussed. Fr. Laurentin had made a suggestion that a provisional cross be erected for the pilgrims coming to the Santa Maria Valley — while awaiting the land for the construction of the permanent cross. His recommendation was posed to Carol; but her answer was "no", a temporary cross could not be erected. Charlie told the group that he and Carol felt everything would eventually be accomplished in God's own time. So everyone understood that for Charlie and Carol, Fr. Laurentin's suggestion had seemingly been put to rest.

The group concluded the meeting with a better awareness of the mixed perspectives among those present, and a number of misunderstandings were appeased. The leaders all agreed that another public meeting for "Bringing Believers Together" should take place under Monsignor Rohde's direction in the future. In the meantime, a mutual acceptance of unity in diversity would be continued as harmoniously as possible. The group recognized how deep the river of intricate problems in Santa Maria ran, but the solutions would take some time to unfold through more praying, waiting, discerning and reconciling. At least, it seemed that Monsignor Rohde had facilitated another step towards peace and unity among the many competent, energetic leaders in the community.

Responses, Warnings and More Questions

The following day, Charlie wrote a letter to Monsignor Rohde commending the meeting for the leaders, as well as for the community. He also made an apology for his mishandling of Barbara:

September 3, 1992

Dear Monsignor Rohde,

The meeting last night at the Castro's home was of extreme importance to God's people of Santa Maria and perhaps to His people of the world. Under your spiritual guidance and direction, many hearts were touched and transformed into a more peaceful and loving attitude. Great progress towards unity and harmony within this valley was witnessed, in our opinion, by all that attended. This feeling of working together and in cooperating with each other, that was well established during this meeting, will radiate out to many others. Let us pray that Satan will not destroy the good that began last night. We sincerely thank both you and Father Rene Laurentin for your efforts in helping to bring believers together.

Regarding the public meeting on Saturday, August 22, 1992, we saw a sincere attempt on your part and the supporters of this meeting to begin the unification of this valley. Many questions and doubts were eliminated and many mis-conceptions put to rest. We are looking forward to the next public meeting. Please let us know the exact time and place so we can support it. We will pray for its success as was done for the first one.

Please accept my apology for any part of the misunderstandings and confusion that might have arisen due to our mishandling of the situation with Barbara. As you stated, this business of apparitions, how to work with and interrupt messages, was something very new to all of us. After viewing the testing and indepth work done to verify an apparition, I will henceforth leave that responsibility of verification to the experts. Our complete focus will be on the mission of building the "Cross of Peace" as asked for by Mary in her messages to Carol...

Charlie and Carol Nole
Cross of Peace Project
[Letter of September 3, 1992]

The apology to Monsignor Rohde was admirable and perhaps some day the wounds will heal to a point that it can be personally extended to Barbara as well.

Two weeks later a public notice was issued by the Cross of Peace Corporation inviting supporters to work in peace and harmony, but there were also some clear warnings

September 22, 1992

To whom it May Concern:

The Cross of Peace Project Corporation Board of Directors has reaffirmed five of its key principles at their September 1992 Board meeting:

1. The supporters of the Cross of Peace Project and its mission invite and welcome all their brothers and sisters in Christ, who wish to work in unity and harmony, to join with them that are preparing for His return.

2. The Cross of Peace project mission is first, the spreading of the teachings of Jesus Christ and the Gospel messages of peace, hope and love as especially reflected in the Cross of Peace Messages and second, overseeing the development and construction of the Cross of Peace itself. To this end, the Corporation has established a ministry that focuses on the teachings of

*Jesus Christ as manifest in Holy Scripture and rein-
forced in the Cross of Peace messages. These Cross
messages were reportedly received through the Virgin
Mary, from our Lord, during the period from March
24, 1988, through September 2, 1988. All the messages for the building for the Cross of Peace were
received by Carol Nole of Santa Maria.*

*3. The name of the Cross of Peace is registered as a
private religious corporation under the laws of the State
of California and the United States. No one may use
the name "Cross of Peace" referencing themselves or
any other group (such as a Cross of Peace representa-
tive, locutionist, messenger or visionary) without the
expressed written consent of the Board of Directors of
the Cross of Peace Corporation.*

*4. The Cross of Peace Project takes a neutral
position concerning the authenticity of the many other
alleged visions, locutions, apparitions and messages
that have been reportedly received for the Cross Project.*

*5. Regarding any other crosses being built here in
Santa Maria Valley, or elsewhere, by any other group,
we feel it is solely a matter for those who wish to build
them. However, the "Cross of Peace" name will not be
allowed to be used by anyone else for any other cross,
either temporary or permanent. The name is registered
with the State and Federal Government and is assigned
to our religious corporation. Mary told us that we must
have patience in doing Her Son's work. The land that
Mary designated for Her Son's cross will become available in God's time, not ours. We must continue to do as
Mary has asked of us so many times......pray, pray,
pray.* [Public Notice, Cross of Peace Corporation,
September 22, 1992.]

Temporary Cross Rejected

It was also clear through this public notice that Fr.
Laurentin's suggestion may not have been taken in the

spirit that it was intended. He first made the suggestion in a public letter, addressed to the "Believers" assembled at the August 22nd unity meeting, then again to the various prayer group leaders on September 2, 1992. His intent was to help unify the community under a provisional Cross. He held the opinion that it would be permissible to have a temporary place for the pilgrims to come and pray, while awaiting the permanent site designated by the Virgin Mary on highway 166. He suggested a location in the Santa Maria hills — away from the traffic — that would accommodate large crowds of people and be conducive to prayer. Fr. Laurentin said he did not believe a temporary site would compromise being true to Carol's messages nor would it pose a theological problem. He considered that the primary essence of Our Lady's message to the people of Santa Maria through Carol was to build a Cross.

Finally, the notice also made it clear to the people that since the Cross of Peace organization is legally a private religious corporation, its board has the option of not taking suggestions made by theologians, the community or Church Authority.

Once again, this type of announcement left a pivotal question in the minds of many people.

The confusion in Santa Maria has often revolved around the organizational structure of the Cross of Peace Project. It is not a ministry formed under the umbrella of a Catholic Parish nor under Canon Laws that pertain to Catholic Associations. It is an autonomous California non-profit corporation that has the right under the law to function as it chooses in meeting its non profit intent. The faithful of the Catholic Church should not be misled into thinking otherwise. If the people in Santa Maria had understood this from the very beginning, perhaps, the many questions that have surrounded the Cross of Peace could have been cleared up long ago.

Chapter 17

A Time to Plan and Understand

A Shrine in Santa Maria?

Many people have also spoken about the possibility of Cross of Peace becoming one of several Catholic Shrines on the Central Coast. An official Shrine of the Church must be established according to Canon Law and Church norms. The same holds true for a chapel associated with a Catholic Shrine. Therefore, it would be impossible to have the Cross of Peace established as an official Catholic Shrine, independent of the Church.

The Need for Continued Discernment

In Santa Maria, all of these matters await future discussion and interpretation. An ecumenical project may mean that everyone is invited to participate by uniting in the effort to eventually erect the Cross, pray at the site and attend spiritual activities. On May 4, 1988, Our Lady said to Carol, *"...Many will gather to bring this about. Exclude not one of my children."* In this respect, none of the Blessed Mother's Children would ever be "excluded", as Mary is the Mother of All Mankind. But Her message to Carol on April 19, 1988, *"...Let all participate as they are able...,"* might also explain certain limits. Except for very specific circumstances, our separated brothers and sisters who do not accept the fullness of truth and practice of the Catholic faith, must be excluded from receiving the Sacrament of Reconciliation and Eucharist, when those sacraments are celebrated in the Catholic community. Since Our Lady is obedient to the Church, she has full knowledge of Church directives regarding ecumenism and stipulations regulating liturgical worship and the Sacraments. She affirms the Church by reminding us to be obedient to the Holy Father and our bishops who are in union with him.

> Celebration of the Sacraments is an action of the celebrating community carried out within the community, signifying the oneness in faith, worship and life of the community. Where this unity of sacramental faith is deficient, the participation of the separated brethren with Catholics, especially in the sacraments of the Eucharist, penance and anointing of the sick, is forbidden. [Vatican Council II, Decree on Ecumenism, Sharing in Liturgical Worship With Other Separated Brethren, p. 499.]

This exclusion currently exists for our separated brothers and sisters who come to the celebration of the Eucharist at special Cross of Peace functions and the Anniversary Celebrations of Carol Nole's messages.

As the plans for the Cross and the Santa Maria Valley continue to unfold, there will still be much to scrutinize. The great lessons being learned here should be an example for many in the Church, who might also be challenged by the complexities and controversies that surround mystical phenomena. The discernment process takes time and it is not easy to untangle confusion when it arises. But the light will eventually shine from the mountain top in Santa Maria, because Our Lady of the Immaculate Heart will continue to "Bring the Believers Together."

A Jewel in the Mud

As for Barbara, what seems so ironic to me is that there would have been no testing; no interest in Barbara by Fr. Laurentin and Dr. Miravalle; and no books written about her, if the adversaries had not slandered her; called her a fake, crazy and possessed. The people who support and believe in Barbara had noticed her simplicity and childlike ways, but had never made any of the horrible accusations. I imagine that we have to thank the adversaries for stirring the mud and raising the dust, so that we could see the jewel that was hidden there.

Chapter 18

Infinite Moments

Mary of Nazareth is infinitely part of God's Plan. She exists in the fullness of grace from the moment of her conception. So, when we speak of **"Mary's Plan,"** we are really speaking about the plan of the Trinity for reconciling all of creation, and the redemption of all mankind.

Mary is the Connection

Mary's role is unique. In very simple terms she said yes, I will cooperate. She brought Jesus into the world as true man, true God. Thus, she was totally united with the Trinity through the divine person of her Son. In giving birth to Jesus she gave birth to the Source of divine grace.

In her infinite role, Mary perpetually brings mankind to her Son Jesus. Whether we realize it or not, she's the connection uniting us to the Heart of the Trinity. And all this happens through the power and love of the Holy Spirit — through Mary, in the power of the Holy Spirit, to her Son and the Eternal Father.

Those who are Catholics should have a better understanding of her role, but this is often not the case.

I might dare to say that one of the most important parts of Mary's Plan is to arrange divine appointments for meeting her Son. In one way or another she has been arranging appointments for nearly 2,000 years, but in our age, she is extending the invitation in a profound way, and she is calling the whole Family of God. Are we willing to allow her to arrange our schedules, make the appointment and eagerly await the meeting? Do we acknowledge Mary as a Motherly secretary of our souls? If we say no, our hearts are closed, and we may miss the divine appointment of a life time.

The Madonna Comes to Dispel the Darkness

And now, in this very day, she has come from Heaven to earth. Why? Humanity has primarily rejected God through egocentric ideals, practical atheism, drugs, abortion, sexual impurity, materialism and great apostasy in the Church. She has come with her special presence to dispel the darkness and distribute graces; to mother, love and nurture us; to console us in our afflictions; to school us in simplicity, holiness and the gospel life. She has come to teach us to pray. She is pleading with all her children to open their arms and be ready to welcome her Son through a transition of hearts.

Her plan is also to usher in a new Pentecost and the Eucharistic reign of her Son. The stars on her crown are shining with hope and the rays of her Immaculate Heart are penetrating the present darkness that envelopes our souls. It is the time of her Triumph. The head of Satan will be crushed by her heel.

A Great Truth

Mary's Plan is not to draw God's children to herself but to her divine Son who is the source of Eternal Life. Through her Motherhood, can we recognize a great truth? Not only is Mary the way by which God has come to us, but she is also the way by which He wills us to come to Him. Thus, she mediates grace through her role as co-redemptrix. [*Introduction to Mary, The Heart of Marian Doctrine and Devotion, pps. 59-83*]

May We All be One

But she is also warning us to turn from our self-centered ways, because in these times we are on the verge of destroying the very life that God has always intended for us. We must make a choice: the time is now and the time moment is urgent. Mary's Plan is for peace beyond our understanding. She wants us to have peace of heart and mind; peace in families, peace in societies and peace in the world. But most of all, she desires her Son's prayer at the Last Supper to finally be fulfilled:

May they all be one,
just as, Father, you are in me and I am in you,
so that they also may be in us,
so that the world may believe it was you who sent me.
I have given them the glory you gave to me,
that they may be one as we are one.
With me in them and you in me,
may they be so perfected in unity
that the world will recognize that it was you who sent me.

Father,
I want those you have given me
to be with me where I am,
so that they may always see my glory
which you have given me
because you loved me before
the foundation of the world.
[John 17: 21-24 NJB]

Spiritual Center of Peace

In this "Age of Mary," we have seen that her apparitions have been greater than at any other time in the
history of the Church. And now, we seem to find
ourselves rapt in the culmination of these exalted
Marian events. Along with her prolonged appearances
in Medjugorje, she is speaking and appearing in many
other parts of the world as well. These "centers of
Peace," on earth have been chosen by Our Lady for
the distribution of special graces and to make her
intentions known through her messages. They are part
of Mary's Plan.

A Chosen Area

As the reader can see, Santa Maria and the Central
Coast of California have been favored with special
graces for many years — from both Our Lord and Our
Lady. This area of California has no doubt been chosen as a spiritual center of peace. One will also find a
number of seminaries and monasteries dotting the
Central Coast, many which are new: the Camaldolese

Hermitage of the Immaculate Heart, in Big Sur; the Benedictine Monastery of the Risen Christ, Los Osos; the Franciscan Monastery, Oceano; the San Lorenzo Seminary of the Capuchin Franciscans in Santa Ynez; the Discalced Carmel of St. Joseph in Lompoc and the Josephite Seminary in Santa Maria.

Summary

In drawing to a close let us summarize the key points in the history and the messages that have been released thus far:

1842: The Plan Begins?
1. Don Juan Pacifico Ontiveros named the river, his rancho and the nearby mesa after Mary the Mother of Jesus.

1882: The City
1. The city was officially named Santa Maria — Holy Mary.

1883-1976: Missing Elements
1. An unknown period of history to the author, when all of Mary's children cooperated in her Plan.

1976-77: Prophecies in the Prayer Groups
1. The people of the Central Coast are to be a 'light on the mountain top.'
2. 'Many will come from the north and the south to find refuge and solace here.'
3. We are to give spiritual, moral and physical sustenance to those who come — feed, clothe and shelter.

4. Prepare for difficult times to come.
5. Be ready to move as a People of God.
6. Pray, discern and transcend divisions; mutual discernment is not an option but a must; responding to God's word is a priority, not a luxury.
10. Support and submission to leaders in the Church community is a must; discerning and measuring leadership by gifts manifested is essential in prayer groups (not just choosing strong personalities or popular vocal people); expect God to work through the leaders.
11. We must learn how to forgive and make clear agreements.
12. Develop a teaching ministry, and the effects will be known world wide.

1985: Locutions from Jesus
1. Keep interceding; the victory is almost complete.
2. His Mother Mary will be enthroned as Queen of the Valley in the future.
3. Satan will be defeated and the Valley will shine as a beacon for the whole world to see.
4. All who don't believe in the role and power given to the Blessed Mother will believe.

1988: Locutions from Jesus
1. Spread his Mother's message of love, repentance, conversion, fasting, prayer and penance.
2. Teach those who have been blinded by the plans of Satan.
3. Remain in the unity of the Holy Family and many blessings will be seen in your work for family unity.
4. Be united to the Eucharistic Heart of Jesus in Mass celebrated throughout all time.

1988: Locutions from the Blessed Mother

1. Erect a 75 foot Cross on the north side of Santa Maria, on a hill overlooking the Santa Maria Valley, in the area designated by Our Lady; there will be no cost for the land; laborers and funds will be bountiful; the Cross will be a sign of peace and hope acting as a beacon to draw all of her Children to her Son.

2. Many will stay in her City of Peace; The City Council officially designated Santa Maria as The City of Peace June 7, 1988; the people of Santa Maria must be gracious hosts and give their love to others.

3. Our Lady will give signs in the Heavens shower her graces, be in our midst; and gifts will flow.

4. In the future the Santa Maria Valley will be dedicated to the Holy Family.

5. The path is long; some will grow weary, but Our Lady will give them the strength to continue.

6. Her Son will be lifted up with praise and glory when everyone opens their hearts to let the love flow from within.

7. Satan is strong, heal the dissent and don't let him make divisions.

8. The Madonna has the complete plan; all will come about — Pray, Pray, Pray.

1990: Our Lady Appears

1. Her title in Santa Maria is "Our Lady of the Immaculate Heart" and this title pleases her very much.

Chapter 19

Awaiting a New Dawn

Reflecting Jesus: A Cause for Division

It must break the Blessed Mother's heart to see so much division among her children, especially when she is now at the center of disunity. However, Dr. Mark Miravalle sheds a little more light on the big puzzle reminding us: "But in truth, Mary in her doctrine and devotion is a cause for division only when she reflects her Son, the sign of contradiction to the world (cf. Lk 2: 34), and the Body of her Son, the Church, which has been entrusted with safeguarding the revelation of Christ without compromise until He comes again in glory." [Mark Miravalle, STD, *Introduction to Mary*, p. 155.] Mary is reflecting her Son in Santa Maria, and Satan continues to try and stop this reflection and victory that has already been won, by raising as much havoc as possible. But through all the suffering, trials and controversies, the fruits have been evident for nearly seventeen years; the people continue to respond to Mary's Plan. They have never given up, and surely, this must be the greatest sign of authenticity! As the author Michael Brown would stimulate our thoughts, it may well be that we are approaching a decisive "Final Hour."

Challenges

If Mary's Plan for Santa Maria is to move forward everyone must, at least, begin to meet the challenges given to all of us.

To the Bishops:

1. Remember that apparitions represent a phenomenon of faith in the midst of the people of God and the visionaries involved.
2. Be open; test the Spirits and hold on to what is good by examining the fruits.
3. Take an active part in the discernment process by realizing there is a difference between judging and ensuring pastoral care of the faithful.
4. Facilitate peace and unity among the clergy by providing information that will clarify what is happening in Santa Maria; give the clergy guidelines for assisting the people; dispel the idea that pastoring is giving official Church support in these situations.
5. Benefit from reading the Seper Document which outlines established criteria developed by Rome for investigating and judging these events.
6. Provide adequate schooling in mystical theology for seminarians; hold a workshop for the established clergy to facilitate a better understanding of extraordinary charisms and mystical phenomena.

To the Clergy:

1. Be open; do not rush to systematically dissuade and suppress, by charging the faithful with illuminism or collective hysteria, while at the same

time, safeguard faith, morals and the public revelation and church teaching; correct errors.

2. Seek to become informed with the truth not rumors; question those who are most apt to have the correct answers.

3. Examine and Cultivate the fruits by listening to the testimonies, being sensitive to those who give them.

4. Assist Monsignor Rohde in guiding the leaders of the movement in Santa Maria by participating as a team on a regular basis; pray with those who are involved and help reconcile the community.

To the faithful and leaders in Santa Maria:

1. Continue to come together as believers; transcend the divisions and controversies that have existed, by working at the reconciliation process through prayer, forgiveness, communication, and spiritual formation.

2. Recognize that changes and modifications are even part of a project requested by Heaven itself, and they do not compromise the essence of a heavenly message; the faithful are not owners of Our Lady but servants and handmaids, who are cooperating within the human limits of her special plans.

3. Understand that messages given through prayer, special charisms, locutions, visions and apparitions are always filtered through the person receiving the message adding nothing to the public revelation already received. Know that the subjectivity of the locutionist or visionary is always involved, requiring mutual discernment by the People of God.

4. Continue to give witness to the fruits by testimony and dialog with the clergy, Episcopal Vicar, qualified experts, the faithful and the whole Family of God.

5. Mutually discern and ask questions of those who will get the correct answers.
6. Welcome the pilgrims, be good hosts, and pray for their needs.
7. Cooperate with church authority, submitting to obedience when requested.

To the Board of Newhall Land and Farming Company:

1. Forgive the people of Santa Maria and others for being overzealous and intimidating.
2. Dialog with Monsignor Rohde, Episcopal Vicar, to gain a better understanding of the events in Santa Maria.
3. Examine the Williamson Act to see if the provisions would allow the Catholic Church to assume use of the land for a Shrine.
4. Review what happened in 1877 with the little town of La Graciosa, located in the Santa Maria Valley. Ask this question: Might H. M. Newhall wish to cooperate from "his eternal home," with the Mother of Jesus, in welcoming pilgrims to the land on highway 166, rather than evicting them as was done so many years ago at La Graciosa?

Concluding Wisdom of the Wise

In conclusion, it would be admirable for everyone to put into practice what the renown Marian theologian Fr. Rene Laurentin has to say regarding the discernment of the extraordinary events happening in this Century.

Let us take the promptings of Vatican II seriously; let us try to go beyond a purely juridical mentality that would have believers reduced to robots in a permanent state of blind expectancy, practicing blind obedience both before and after the Church's judgement: abstention before the judgment and submission after it. This passivity is diametrically opposed to the freedom of Christian life, because both the faithful and the authorities live by God's Grace and the inspiration of the Spirit. These graces are shared through co-operation in the act of discernment. Problems are overcome by a little self-sacrifice on all sides, so that charity and obedience prevail in an atmosphere of openness and self-criticism. [Rene Laurentin, *Apparitions of the Blessed Virgin Mary Today*, p. 30]

May the messages of "Our Lady of the Immaculate Heart," given through Barbara Matthias, now finally speak for themselves.

PUBLISHER'S PREFACE TO THE MESSAGES

The initial messages from Mary to Barbara Matthias pertain, for the most part, to the people of the Santa Maria Valley. The messages should not be misinterpreted to mean that people who live elsewhere are insignificant to the Blessed Mother. On the contrary, she invites everyone to be close to her, wherever they reside.

The messages given for the public knowledge ordinarily begin with My Child or My Children. Her departing words are usually, "I give you my blessing of Love, Peace and Joy." It is not necessary to print these salutations with each message; therefore, they have been omitted from the text. However, the reader should note that they constitute part of the message.

Barbara sees Mary, speaks with her, and can touch her just as two people on earth would relate to one another; but the event is conditioned in a different dimension — the duration of God. Therefore, Barbara meets the daily apparition of Our Lady.

Locutions mentioned in the narrative of this volume are commonly defined as communications from Heaven (of a mystical nature) that can best be described as an interior voice perceived in the "heart" or intellect of the recipient. However, the voice can also be audible and heard interiorly or exteriorly.

At the time this book was being assembled for printing, announcements were being disseminated from Nancy, in Conyers, Georgia; Denise in Woodland, Ca; Louise in Sacramento, Ca; and Sharon in Orange County, Ca. predicting catastrophic disasters for the United States: some specifically for California.

Any linked predictions emanating from Orange County, Ca. which reference the above four messengers to Santa Maria, are not associated with the Episcopal Vicar of the Santa Barbara Pastoral Region, Barbara Matthias or her meessages in any manner. Neither are they associated with the author, the publisher or the text of *Mary's Plan*

MESSAGES GIVEN TO BARBARA MATTHIAS FROM OUR LADY OF THE IMMACULATE HEART

MARCH 24, 1990 — FEAST OF THE ANNUNCIATION

MESSAGE:

My children, I love you so very much. Have patience, the Cross will be erected here in my Son's time.

I give you my blessing. I know how strong your faith is in my Son and me. Keep doing as I ask. My children, I am giving you graces at this time. This is a time of Mercy and Peace.

Pray the Rosary often — very often. I, your Mother, hold the world and all my children's needs in my Immaculate Heart. Love my Son unconditionally.

Remind people that I am waiting to love them. People ignore My Son and think only of worldly things. He loves them all so much.

March 28, 1990

MESSAGE:

My, children, you have asked about my title. I prefer my title, "The Immaculate Heart". My Immaculate Heart is overlooking all the people in Santa Maria and extending my love and graces to all here. Santa Maria will become a special home of holiness for my Son's people.

You have asked what my Son and I want you to do concerning the project of the Cross. Simply trust that my Son will provide all that is necessary for the project.

You must pray, fast and make reparation for sin. Pray the Rosary.

People who will come to the hill will be blessed. They, and even their relatives, will be transformed into the type of sons and daughters my Son and I desire. Lead holy lives. Do not get tied up with material things. Keep your souls focused on My Son and on your true home — Heaven.

Santa Maria will be a haven of rest for all who come here. There will be great peace and joy here which the world cannot understand.

Love unconditionally and remember — be patient. I love you.

March 31, 1990

MESSAGE:

My children, the messages I am giving are basically what I have said before. It is important for me to remind people of my messages.

Be patient, My Children, the project is going on at the pace that I desire. I know you are anxious, but everything must be done in my Son's time. I am pleased with what you are doing now. Keep praying, fasting and turning your hearts to my Son and me. Pray the Rosary often. Know that I am with you through all of this.

You must keep your hearts open like little children. Be trusting like little children who love and depend on their Mother. I am with you and this project is in my motherly heart. Be at peace. My plans are for peace.

Believe that this project will be a source of holiness for all who desire to love me with their heart and allow my graces to transform their lives. I want my children to receive my graces.

My children, live in my peace and love. I am with you.

April 1, 1990

MESSAGE:

Note: Our Lady was asked by Barbara a second time about her title.

My children, I desire my title to be, Our Lady of the Immaculate Heart. This title pleases me very much. My Immaculate Heart is filled with pure love for the people of Santa Maria and for the great project you have undertaken for me.

Many people will come to Santa Maria. They will come to seek the love and peace that I their Mother will give to them in abundance.

Keep your hearts open to the graces I am pouring out. (Today the people witnessed a great sign in the sky.) It was not by chance or accident that my children noticed the sign of the sun dancing. It was a sign of my love and mercy. It was a sign of the great graces of sanctity I desire to pour out on my people. It was also a sign of my presence and the presence of my Son here in Santa Maria.

The great faith of the people here is one of my greatest consolations. I will always be with my people here and care for them as a true Mother. Keep a humble and serene heart. Rejoice in my presence among you.

Show gratitude to My Son and me by living as we desire. Pray many prayers of gratitude and do not take anything done for you for granted. It is out of pure Love that I turn my heart to you.

The Cross will be a symbol of faith, love and peace. It will be like a magnet attracting hearts and drawing them into the abyss of love and mercy that is in my own heart. If only you could comprehend how very much I love you.

My Children do not grow weary. I will give you the strength and courage to complete the task of this great project for me.

Many souls will be saved here in Santa Maria, if you continue to pray, to fast and to be obedient children. Keep your eyes of faith open to all the beautiful things happening here and give thanks, praise and glory to My Son.

Do not let anything become a stumbling block to the work of the project. Do not lose perseverance, faith or trust. Pray the Rosary. Each bead of the Rosary, said with a sincere and loving heart, is a flower of love to me.

April 2, 1990

MESSAGE:
Pray for my priests, my children. They are consecrated to me. Pray for them even when they make mistakes. This is when they need your prayers. Satan tries hard to deceive them because they are consecrated to my Son and are dear to Him. The way is not

easy for my priests, for they are in a battle against Satan. I, the Mother of Priests, will care for them, but your prayers are necessary too.

Do not worry about what others think of you for following my requests in carrying out this project. Some will work against you and not understand, but you must stand firm and do all I ask.

Satan seeks to ruin the carrying out of this project. Do not allow this to make you fearful. I will triumph and the Cross will shine forth as a sign of victory over Satan and his followers. Pray much for the defeat of Satan.

I point toward Heaven. I want to remind you to work towards your heavenly home by making daily sacrifices. Accepting things that are hard for you to endure helps you to grow spiritually. When you make sacrifices for me, you grow in virtue and show that you are humble and trusting. Be humble. I am an example of humility. Follow my example.

Remember, your love for one another is a sign to others that this project is from me. Therefore, do not be judgmental or harsh with each other concerning the things of this project, but work in harmony and love towards it's completion.

My Children, I give you my peace. Let this peace reign in your hearts.

April 3, 1990

MESSAGE:
The people of Santa Maria must care about making reparation. The sins of man are too numerous and horrifying. The people of Santa Maria must be ex-

amples of holiness to all people, thus, consoling my heart. Make reparation for the sins of man and tell others to stop offending my Son.

Speak out boldly against all that is wrong. Do not be afraid to stand up firmly against the powers of evil. Do not compromise with the world, the flesh and the devil. Do not grow lax in serving my Son and me as this will give Satan a chance to work on you.

I want Santa Maria to be different than most other places. I want no heart in Santa Maria to be closed to my Son's desires and wishes.

I have chosen Santa Maria to be a place pleasing to my Son. Let its inhabitants live as an example of me, whose name your city bears. My children, my desire is for peace. Help me bring this peace to others by the example of your lives.

Do not stand by idly where souls need to be saved. The people of Santa Maria must be instruments in the Heart of my Son to bring about the peace I desire. This peace only comes from living pure and holy lives and by pleasing Jesus, your Lord.

April 4, 1990

MESSAGE:
(Today Mary had twelve stars around her head.) My Children, these twelve stars symbolize the twelve Apostles. You are modern day apostles who must live the Gospel life by following the example of my Son on earth. You must walk in His footsteps and be willing to be persecuted just as He was persecuted. You must be willing to be persecuted for loving Him. Make Santa Maria a holy place.

(Mary had a rose imprinted on the front of the gown she was wearing.) This rose and its fragrance symbolize the beautiful fragrance that arises to my Son and me when you in Santa Maria are faithful to prayer, fasting, sacrifices and the Rosary.

My children, I see Santa Maria as a place of preparation for Heaven. The people of Santa Maria must be good teachers and prophets, spreading my messages and speaking out through the power of the Holy Spirit.

My Children in Santa Maria, seek the gifts and fruit of the Holy Spirit in all that you do. These gifts and fruit will enable you to carry out the plans for the project. Seek the Holy Spirit's guidance. Pray to the Holy Spirit each day.

When I look down on Santa Maria and your valley, I see a City of Peace and hope. I see many souls filled with hope. This pleases My Heart and brings me great consolation. I desire that this peace and hope be spread throughout the world. Nothing is impossible, if you trust in me. I desire all of you to reach your heavenly home. Keep hope! (When the Blessed Mother said this I saw an arch of light surround her. It was dazzling and beautiful to behold.)

I want Santa Maria to be like a small preview of Heaven. You have all the graces I can give. Use them wisely. Do not push any grace I give you aside. Each grace is like a seed that has been planted and it must be nurtured.

April 5, 1990

MESSAGE:

It is for love of you that I come to bring peace and to reign as Queen and Mother in Santa Maria.

My Children, tell people to rejoice. Know that because I am with you, no harm will come to you. You will face many trials, but no harm will come to you. Be calm amidst the disasters, distractions and trials of this world. The people of Santa Maria are a people who live in the world, but they must not be of the world. Remember this and remain calm. This will show that you are truly my children.

I want Santa Maria to be like a bridge which leads to Heaven. Stay obedient to my wishes and Santa Maria will be known for its holiness not only nation-wide but worldwide.

April 6, 1990

MESSAGE:

My Children, I want the Hill of Peace to be conse-crated to My Immaculate Heart.

Santa Maria is dear to Jesus and me. We have anointed your Valley as holy ground. You must live in holiness from the depths of your hearts.

Be a people of hope and live each day as a day of joy. You the people of Santa Maria are an Alleluia people.

I desire a modern day Pentecost in Santa Maria. This is possible for those who have faith.

Your Lady of the Immaculate Heart is so filled with love for you. Allow my love to make you feel secure and serene. I have chosen you as my own.

Remember that the Heavenly Father sees and knows all that you do, think and say. Let your attitudes be not like those of the unbelievers, who think the things of this world will last forever. Accept all the graces you are given for the Glory of my Son and the Heavenly Kingdom.

My Children in Santa Maria, your love for each other must be so strong that the world will know you belong to me.

My Children, this is to be your major weapon against Satan and the evils of the world. (With this Mary held up Her beautiful Rosary.)

I am with you always and I give you my blessing of Love, Peace and Joy.

April 7, 1990

MESSAGE:

My Children, I desire peace in my valley. Why is there dissention among some of you? I desire that you reconcile any dissention. I know if the desire of your soul is really to reconcile. Be sincere — you cannot deceive your Mother.

Do not let gossip or envy enter your hearts. This is not to be a part of what I want in Santa Maria. Do not judge each other or think that anyone of you is better than another.

Forget selfishness! Do not let your egos become a hindrance to coming into My Heart and to the plans I desire for the project. Follow the example of My Son who was always selfless and cared for others.

I desire that you fast, especially on Wednesdays and Fridays. For those who are sick and cannot fast, a modified fast will please me. I will look at their good intentions. Those who fast on Wednesdays and Fridays should fast on bread and water.

Remember to sacrifice those things that really are hard to give up. Abound in acts of charity. God is Love; and where Love abounds, there My Son abides.

Use the gift of wisdom in carrying out the plan for the completion of the project. Using true wisdom is a step towards the completion of the project. Invoke the Holy Spirit.

I am the White Lily of your valley, and I desire that this valley be pure. Remove anything which will hinder you on the way to Heaven.

Consider the example of Your Mother in all your endeavors, and follow unreservedly the Will of My Son. Be patient and continue in my love.

Come to Me with open hearts. Do not give lip service to your prayers. Mean what you are saying in each word of each prayer you pray. This is very important to me.

It gratifies My Heart to have people come together in the unity. Remember, My children of Santa Maria, that you are temples of the Holy Spirit. You must have your hearts open to His gifts and fruit. Do nothing to grieve the Holy Spirit.

Consider the beauty of your Valley and praise God who created everything you see in the Valley of Peace. Take time to appreciate the things of the Lord. His creations are beautiful and meant to make you happy and to Glorify Him.

I give you my blessing of Love, Peace and Joy; and I plead for you to keep coming to me in prayer, love and service. Your Mother is always there to help you.

(The Blessed Mother came today with the Infant Jesus and two small angels, one on each side of her.)

April 8, 1990 (Palm Sunday)

MESSAGE:

It is one of the greatest joys of My Heart to be among my people in Santa Maria. Will you keep welcoming me with love?

My desire is to be totally united with you, so that in all you do, you will feel my presence with you — as you pray and as you serve me by doing all I ask. You will even know I am present in your homes. This is to be a special blessing for my people of Santa Maria. Let my presence give you security and hope in a troubled world.

As you experience my presence, a deeper and deeper peace will come upon each and every one of you. This peace will be a heavenly peace.

My Children of Santa Maria, remember your future is in my hands and the hands of Jesus. Sometimes you tend to want to be in charge. Do not presume that you have control of things. Jesus and I are in complete control.

My Children, My son is the potter and you, my children of Santa Maria, are the clay. Even now you are being molded and formed. When you are finished being molded, Santa Maria will shine like a beacon of light, leading to the Hearts of Jesus and Your Immaculate Mother who stands before you.

April 9, 1990

MESSAGE:

My Children of Santa Maria, I am pleading with you to console the pain I feel over the condition of the world. Live as My Son desires. You must not forsake the Gospel Life He has given you. (Tears were profusely running down the cheeks of Blessed Mother).

My Children, keep praying that the people of the United States will cease to commit the offenses and crimes which they continue to do willfully and which offend My Son so deeply.

My Children, you my chosen flock of Santa Maria must be willing to be brave soldiers in the battle already being waged against us. In the end we will win, but strong perseverance is necessary until the victory. The evil forces are deceitful and treacherous and turn hearts against My Son. Are you willing to help fight this battle with all the powers of your soul?

My Children, in carrying out my plans for peace and for the project, be concerned about putting each decision you make in the Heart of the Holy Trinity. The Eternal Father, whose all powerful and holy wisdom foresees your needs, will take care of His Children as a good Father.

Our Jesus has paid the price for your salvation by redeeming you. His love will be extended through the project of the Cross. The Holy Spirit will shower you with His gifts and fruit. Your souls must be receptive. Remember I choose for you to have a New Pentecost in Santa Maria.

April 10, 1990

MESSAGE:

My Children, the community of Santa Maria must be a radiant example of charity shining forth for all to see and follow.

Do not let any pettiness stir up disturbances among you. You must live in harmony. I am a Mother of Peace and I desire peace in Santa Maria — a sacred peace which comes from living as brothers and sisters in the footsteps of Jesus.

April 11, 1990

MESSAGE:

My Children, a sign of my presence among you is that you be wholly transformed. Persevere. Remember My Son's promise: His yoke is easy and His burden is light.

I am Queen of the Universe — the whole universe — and yet I have chosen to be here with you. What does this say about my Love for you?

(Mary wore a beautiful crown and jewels were inlaid on the bottom of her gown. The numerous sparkling jewels were brilliant and beautiful.) My Child each of these priceless jewels on my gown symbolize the individual virtues pouring out from the lives of my children in Santa Maria.

I assure the people of Santa Maria, that if they continue to progress in virtue and holiness, peace will increase in their hearts. Seek the Kingdom of Heaven. (Mary then pointed toward Heaven and said) Oh, Santa Maria, keep living as My Son and I desire.

My Children, I have so many different and individual personalities among my children. Each of you is unique. A beautiful garden has many different kinds of flowers, and so it is with you my children.

I give you my blessing of Love, Peace and Joy and My sweet assurance that I am with you always. Keep your hearts peaceful and holy. I love you so much.

April 12, 1990 — Holy Thursday

MESSAGE:

My children, pray and remember Our Lord's passion and death. The Apostles scattered when Jesus was arrested and made to go on the Way of the Cross. You, my children who are modern day apostles, must not scatter like scared sheep, but must unite in prayer.

My child, see this light radiating from Me. (There were rays of light shining forth from Blessed Mother.) Let these rays remind my Children, to radiate the Love and Peace of Jesus and Your Lady of the Immaculate Heart to all the world.

My Child, My Son is here with me today, and He wants to let you know His Blessings are on the project and on all Our Chosen Ones of Santa Maria. He asks that you abandon yourselves to Him, and that you love and obey me also. (Mary had Baby Jesus in Her Arms.)

My Children, Do not be afraid of any crosses which are sent your way. Each time you carry a cross bravely, silently and with no complaining, you help Jesus. Love and embrace the Cross, for without a Cross there can be no crown.

Each of you must spend a great deal of time in prayer. The union of your prayers reaches the throne of Your Heavenly Father and are joined to my intercession for the success of the project of the Cross. We must join in prayer, my children, so that the time for the completion of the project which is determined by My Son will come soon.

There is still too much gossip and too many negative things said among my children of Santa Maria. Do not forget to look into yourself first. None of you is perfect. Therefore, none of you has the right to speak against your brother or sister. Treat each other as you would like to be treated.

Do not let anything or anyone confuse you. When your hearts are mine, you are on the sure path to Heaven. I am the Shining Star pointing the way to My Son.

My Children, each day that I am with you I draw you closer to me. It pleases me to remain in Santa Maria and to come to the hill of peace because you are sincere in your love for me.

April 13, 1990 — Good Friday

MESSAGE:
My Children, in you my chosen ones, I see a prophetic people. Tell others about the Gospel life they must live. Encourage them to live this Gospel life to the fullest. Cry out the way to my Son through me.

You have been selected to be children of Your Heavenly Mother. This is a great challenge when the allures of the world, flesh and the devil try to tempt you. Do not give into them. Your Mother is stronger than all the powers of evil. Cling to me when temptations press hard upon you. I understand, for I lived on this earth and was tempted also.

Keep cultivating the field of your hearts. Prune out all undesirable attitudes and vices. Pure hearts will be the greatest gift you can give My Son for Easter — Hearts full of love and holiness. If you do this, you will be pure Easter lilies for Jesus and your Mother.

In your homes, keep the same Spirit your Mother gives to you on the hill of peace. Let no dissensions arise in your homes. Be patient and loving towards all members of your families. Your heavenly home is a home of love and peace, so prepare for your heavenly home by making your earthly homes like the Holy Family's home was in Nazareth.

My Children of Santa Maria, take time to make sure your children learn the true value of Gospel living. Little children can be easily influenced. Make sure they are influenced on the straight and narrow path to Heaven. Help these little ones — so precious in my eyes — to maintain their sweet innocence.

My Immaculate Heart is so grieved by the abortions being performed. It is a modern day slaughtering of the innocents. Tell people abortion is murder. It is a sin which must be stopped. Instruct people in the evils of abortion.

My Children of Santa Maria, be a righteous people in these times of great sin. Like Noah and his family were aided by My Son during the punishment of the great flood, you, my children, are being preserved, protected and led towards sanctity in a time of unrest, worldliness and confusion. Keep your hearts close to Jesus and me.

Honor the dignity of each individual. Each person is being transformed in different ways toward my Son and me. We know each heart and transform each individual. We know the way each heart will be transformed.

My Children, as more and more people come to Santa Maria, I desire that more and more men and women will also seek a priestly and religious vocation. Those who are called to this vocation must be unselfish and follow their calling.

My Children, there is peace in the Valley of Peace. Maintain this peace in your hearts. Do not ever let evil forces try to discourage you from the completion of the project. Your holy goal is to work toward its completion, but in doing so, maintain serenity in your hearts.

I give you My Blessing of Love, Peace and Joy and a smile to warm your hearts. Live on in My Love.

April 14, 1990 — Holy Saturday

MESSAGE:

My Children, do not let your Easter Joy and Hope diminish.

I plead with you to keep your hearts open to prayer, fasting and abandonment to the Holy Spirit. Do not think these things are too hard for you. All you have to do is ask me to help you.

Prepare yourselves for Easter Day by reading Scripture — especially the account of the resurrection of my Son.

My Children, thank you for staying with me for such a long time.

April 15, 1990 — Easter Sunday

MESSAGE:

My children, I want you to give glory to God. You are a "resurrected people" through the transformation of your lives, and you give much happiness and consolation to My Son.

Today my Son won victory over death. Each one of you will live with us in Heaven, if you continue climbing the spiritual ladder to Heaven. This ladder is composed of prayer, penance, sacrifices, fasting and love. Keep climbing the ladder. You will conquer spiritual death through following the gospel life. Persevere.

I have the Child Jesus with Me today. Easter is a very special time for Him, and He wanted to share this sacred time with you. How precious you are to us.

Let Easter be everyday for you. Don't think of Easter as a passing celebration. Live it everyday in your hearts. This is my desire for you.

I give you my blessing of Love, Peace and Joy and the encouragement to persevere in goodness. (Mary and the Infant Jesus blessed each of us.)

April 16, 1990

MESSAGE:

My Children...Now is a time of Mercy; tell people who are away from Jesus and me to turn their hearts back to us immediately. We want all to be saved ... Woe to souls who have abandoned us deliberately and remain in this state. Warn them — tell them before it is too late. It will be horrifying for them. Concern yourselves with living each moment as if it were the last moment you have here to do our will.

My Child, see the doorway to Heaven. (At this time Mary showed me a door to Heaven.) The secret to opening this door is to love me, remain faithful and avoid the things of the world which are hindrances to Eternal Life in Heaven.

My Children, when you realize the seriousness of the end times, and realize that the fate of those against us is eternal, you will see how gracious your Mother is in bringing you close to her and protecting you.

In the end times there will be family dissensions. Members of families will hate each other, quarrel and plan evil for each other. This will be the work of Satan. You, my children, must not let dissensions arise in your families. You must avoid the work of Satan which seeks to enter your hearts and homes. I will protect you. Ask for my graces to overshadow you and your request will be granted.

I have accounted the seriousness of the end times, so that it will be a time of victory for you, if you are faithful.

Note: Today during the apparition I saw the door to Heaven three times and I was also shown a ladder to Heaven two times. Mary was very concerned about our salvation and showing us the way.

April 17, 1990

MESSAGE:
My Children, hold on to the practical advice I have been giving to you. Hold every word I say as important

and urgent. This caring direction from your Lady of the Immaculate Heart is for your lives, and to direct you to Heaven forever.

The power of the Holy Spirit is with us. You my children, belong to the Holy Spirit and to me. Let us band together in prayer. Through your prayers, sacrifices, and fasting the project of the Cross will be completed.

My Children, the test you are going through now is making you grow stronger spiritually. It is making you depend more on Jesus and me and not yourselves. You do need us don't you? You cannot do it alone! We want you to depend on us and to understand that we will help you. Do not be afraid of your littleness in comparison to Jesus. He knows you are only human and loves you as you are.

Keep a joyful spirit among yourselves. You have every reason to be joyful. You have your Mother with you. You are being directed toward Heaven. You have my love and the love of Jesus. You will be given everything you need.

My Children, guard every word that comes out of your mouths. Do not use vulgar and sarcastic language. You are accountable for everything you say. Say only what you would say if Jesus and I were standing before you. We are with you and know every word coming from your lips. Be careful not to displease us by using language unfitting of a Christian.

(Today during the apparition, for a short while there was a huge host in the sky over Blessed Mother's Head. The two little angels of the Cross project were with Her and venerating Her — one on each side of Her.)

April 18, 1990

MESSAGE:

My Children, what are you doing in my Valley of Peace for those who are homeless and those suffering from social injustices? I want you to help people in situations like this.

My Children, never go to bed at night harboring any ill feeling towards your brother or sister. If anything needs to be worked out to further the cause of peace, then arrive at a peaceful understanding while it is still daylight.

April 19, 1990

MESSAGE:

My Children, Pray much for world peace. Peace must be in your hearts before it can be extended to people of other nations. I have been appearing and have given you this peace. Now extend this peace to the world through your prayers for world peace.

Have courage during this time of exile on earth. Live your time here as if you were already in Heaven.

Do not worry about the future of your families. I assure you, your families will be taken care of. They will have an abundance of what they need. My children will be so spiritually rich that they will be beautiful reflections of Jesus and me. So, be content. Concern yourselves only with doing what is pleasing to My Son and me. Do not worry about what others think.

Keep praying the Rosary. I have given the Rosary to you. Pray it with great love. Some complain about the prayers of the Rosary as being repetitious. This complaint is unjustified in My Heart. When you truly love, it will not be boring. Pray it with love because each word of the Rosary is sacred.

My Children, I extend to you great Love, Peace and Joy and a special blessing from my Son and the angels. (Mary, the Child Jesus and the angels all blessed us in unison. Mary gave such a smile of love that it seemed to extend to the whole world.)

April 20, 1990

MESSAGE:

My Children, notice the beauty of our Valley of Peace. This beauty is to be there for you always. Your valley will always be beautiful to behold.

Be on guard, do not lead one another into temptation to sin. If you know your brother or sister has a particular weakness, do not put stumbling blocks in their way.

In all you do, avoid pretentiousness and hypocrisy. Remember when Jesus lived on this earth, He forgave sinners, but spoke out very harshly against hypocrites. Maintain a true heart.

My Children, you are very concerned about the future. Leave the future to Jesus and me. You must cooperate with us, because the plans are in our keeping. We want to take care of you.

Your Mother wants all of you to accept a special grace of fortitude. You must be strong because the devil hates me and my plans for peace. Therefore, continue your prayers to St. Michael the Archangel. Wear the St. Benedict Medal. This medal has the power of exorcism attached to it.

My Children, young people must be respectful to their parents. I want none of my chosen youth to grieve their parents by disrespect. Follow the example of respect shown to Joseph and me by Jesus in our home at Nazareth.

April 21, 1990

MESSAGE:

My intentions are always for the good of your souls. Be patient when you don't understand why I ask something of you.

April 22, 1990

MESSAGE:

My Children, I always want you to be happy. True happiness is where the heart is. You will find happiness in Jesus and me. Give us all of your love and you will always be happy. Without us you cannot be truly happy.

My Children, since the Triumph of Our Hearts is so important, please see to it that your homes are enthroned to Our Hearts.

April 23, 1990

MESSAGE:

My Children, I have been preparing you in so many ways for when the Cross will be erected. The Cross is a symbol of courage and life for all the world.

Do you realize that in cleaving to Jesus and me, the evil forces who attempt to block our plans for peace cannot touch us?

April 24, 1990

MESSAGE:

I, your Lady of the Immaculate Heart, have been with you here in a special way. Since I have been with you, I have taken each of you and changed your life in some very important ways. Each person touched by My Grace is touched so they can become more united to the cause of the project of the Cross. I know where each person is needed in helping with the project. I give the graces for each person to work in doing exactly what I want. Each person is a unique link in the completion of the project.

My Children, the spiritual life is often like a puzzle. All the pieces come together although they are of different shapes and sizes. My Chosen Ones, your spiritual life for me is meant to be like the pieces of a puzzle. No two days of happenings will be exactly the same, and yet all these happenings, different as they are, help to complete the puzzle which is the holy project you have undertaken.

Some of you have been working so hard to get things done that you have not taken time to smile and relax. Give genuine smiles more often.

I would like you to visit the sick in their homes and in the hospitals. Your presence and love can make the difference in their recovery. By visiting the sick, you will bring Jesus and me to them. Some of them have no one to care for them. Do not neglect them.

Pray for the needs of those in prison. Many in prison have not been loved. Through your prayers, those in prison can come to know Jesus and Me. Then they will become free in soul even though they are physically imprisoned.

(**Note:** The Blessed Mother was dressed in a Mexican style gown today. It was similar to the one she wore in Guadalupe.)

April 25, 1990

MESSAGE:
My Children, you are dear to me and precious in my sight.

In other parts of the world there is a great spiritual unrest which saddens me. The world is in turmoil now because in many places Jesus and I have been forgotten. So many people seek after things which are so unnecessary and wrong. Pray, because these souls must awaken quickly before it is too late. They must turn their hearts back to Jesus and me. The time is shorter than they realize.

Console Me in my sadness by remaining faithful to me and all that I have taught you.

Satan is angry because many of you are growing in holiness. He is waging a battle against us. He will try to put disharmony among you and to stir up petty grievances. He will try to bring discouragement to your hearts. Do not fall for him. There is nothing to be discouraged about.

My Immaculate Heart will triumph over Satan. I will crush his head, and then my children will not be bothered by him any longer. The devil has caused much pain. I want you to pray that the Triumph of My Immaculate Heart comes soon.

My Children, banish from your hearts any restlessness. I know you are anxious for things to be completed. You have been doing well with patience. Do not give up patience now. Things are progressing better even than you realize.

A battle, which will be waged by evil forces in the future, will be waged because Satan knows you are going to be successful in your efforts to complete my project and have my messages released. Things take time, but we will be successful. The devil cannot stand sensing this upcoming success.

Say more prayers to defeat the work of Satan.

My Children, I want you to cultivate in your hearts a hatred for evil and a love of good. Then you will be able to discern from the Holy Spirit those things which should be accepted or rejected in your daily life.

I know there are many among you who are going through spiritual and temporal struggles. Do not feel overcome by these struggles. They are temporary. I plead for you. Remember that after every storm there is a rainbow.

I have asked St. Michael the Archangel to keep watch over you. (St. Michael was at the right side of the Blessed Mother today. He looked very strong and able to help defend us against evil.)

April 26, 1990

MESSAGE:

I would like you to say fifteen decades of the Rosary daily so all my plans for peace will go smoothly. These plans will go smoothly if you do as I ask.

Some of you have been neglecting frequent confession because you are so busy. Do not do this, my children. Make time to keep your souls pure temples of the Holy Spirit.

April 27, 1990

MESSAGE:

My Children, your Mother is concerned about people who do not pray the Rosary because they do not know how. Will you please teach people how to pray this beautiful prayer? I don't want anyone to be deprived of the graces received from the prayer of the Rosary. For those who teach others how to pray the Rosary, I have promised to come for them at the hour of their death and that there will be many conversions in their families.

April 28, 1990

MESSAGE:

My children, the way to peace is not through selfishness. Human nature can be too selfish. Selfishness leads to destruction. Rise above your human nature, my children, and share in the divine life of Jesus. Then you will know true peace.

April 29, 1990

MESSAGE:

My children, I have been calling you to Christian perfection. It is an everyday endeavor to reach Christian perfection. For the rest of your life on earth this will be a goal. Never feel that you have completely mastered Christian perfection while living on this earth.

Sometimes direction is hard to take if arrogance stands in the way. You are to be docile to me and to those I put in authority over you. Remember you are sheep not goats. Get rid of your stubbornness.

My Children, you can not conceive of the love Jesus has for you. Without His constant divine providence over you, you would not even have the Cross project in Santa Maria. This divine providence has been given to you by Jesus and me. Thank Him that you have me with you.

April 30, 1990

MESSAGE:

(**Note:** Our Lady brought St. Joseph with her today. This was the first time that St. Joseph appeared with Mary.)

My Children I desire you to make St. Joseph your patron of our Cross project just as Your Mother of the Immaculate Heart is your patroness.

My Children, I would like a Chapel to be built on the hill of peace. I want all to come and Worship my Son and to venerate me, your Mother.

When I spoke about Portugal, I said the faith of the people would always be strong there. Now, I have the privilege of being able to tell you that the same promise is being made to my Children in Santa Maria. The faith will always be strong here. Your Mother has promised this.

May 1, 1990

MESSAGE:
My Children, I desire that Stations of the Cross be placed on the hill of peace when the Cross is erected. I want the Stations of the Cross to be of white material.

I desire one extra Station to be erected along with the original fourteen. Make the fifteenth Station the Resurrection.

My Children, when you have erected the chapel on the hill of peace, please call it The Chapel of the Immaculate Heart of Mary.

I desire that it be built large enough to hold many people — as many people as will come from all destinations. Let it have windows of light. We are a people of "Light."

May 2, 1990

MESSAGE:
My Children, Your Lady of the Immaculate Heart has chosen to stay with you longer than in most places because I am pouring my mercy upon you in abundance.

My Children, you must have a daily Mass and frequent confessions at the chapel on the Hill of Peace.

Their should be an adequate number of priests to hear confessions.

Because of the beautiful scenery on the Hill of Peace, when weather permits, people should have an option of going to confession out of doors or in the chapel. Provide for this option.

Let the stations of the Cross lead to the chapel and call its path The Pathway to Peace.

My Children Your Lady of the Immaculate Heart chooses to stay with you longer than in most places because I am pouring my Mercy upon you in abundance.

I want no soul to be lost. So, I spend much time giving advice that will help save your souls.

May 3, 1990

MESSAGE:
My children, until you reach your goal use much prudence in all you do and say. The time will come when you will look back at all you've been through with great relief and thanksgiving because you will have reached your goal. Until you reach your goal use much prudence and much diplomacy in all your dealings concerning the Cross project. Accept the Holy Spirit's gift of wisdom and understanding which He pours out. You will need these two gifts. I give you this advice because I want you to use these gifts properly. Do not abuse any gift you have received. Be patient with my Motherly advice.

May 4, 1990

MESSAGE:

My Children, magnify the Lord with me. My soul magnifies the Lord, so should yours. When someone looks at you they should see Jesus, just by looking at you. They should thirst for holiness.

The harvest is ripe for reaping. Will you help harvest souls for Jesus? Now is the time for winning souls to the Merciful Heart of Jesus and to my Immaculate Heart.

When the chapel is erected, the Infant Jesus has requested that I ask you to have a statue of the Infant of Prague in the chapel. This will not only honor his childhood, but He promises a special blessing of protection for the chapel for having this statue there.

My children, honor the Most Blessed Trinity; say special prayers and sing special songs. I am the way to Jesus and the Blessed Trinity. It is the Blessed Trinity who allows me to be here with you. There is a fountain of life being poured out from me to you. If you desire to live, come to the water of salvation who is in my heart — my Son Jesus. Drink until your thirst is quenched.

May 5, 1990

MESSAGE:

My children, as soon as the messages are released more people will come, some will even come from other nations of the world. Be open to other races, cultures and traditions.

Let your father Abraham be an example of the faith you need to continue and complete the work of this holy project. He went by faith to another country that was given to him and his descendants. He set out not even knowing where he was going but trusted that God would lead him. Thus, it must be with you. Trust that Jesus and I have led you for a specific purpose and you will be taken care of as Abraham was.

May 6, 1990

MESSAGE:

My children, I the Vessel of Honor, have come to you with love and gratitude. After the chapel is built, pray before the Blessed Sacrament. I desire the Blessed Sacrament be exposed for a certain amount of time daily. When all of your work for the completion of the project comes to an end we shall have a celebration and an anniversary celebration every year thereafter.

May 7, 1990

MESSAGE:

My children, I am like a beacon's light, and I always want to light the way to my Son. Just as a beacon's light shines the way to shore for ships on the sea when it is dark, so do I light the way to Jesus in a world that is full of the darkness of sin. I want my children to live in my light.

My children you are modern day apostles. When I call you, do not hesitate. My desire is for you to become spiritually strong. Remember a good mother only gives to her children what is good. So it is with your Heavenly Mother.

May 8, 1990

Message:
My children, Your Mother of the Immaculate Heart greets you with fondest love. I see among you, a people of great faith. I desire that your faith spread all over the world. This faith, which begins in your hearts, will spread worldwide by your example. Make a profession of faith daily. Be courageous and stand firm in facing the challenge this profession involves. It is an eternal profession, for life in Heaven will profess to the Glory of God.

Wear my Brown Scapular. I promise that whoever wears the Scapular will receive Eternal Life in Heaven. There are three things which keep the devil away: the Holy Name of Jesus, the Rosary and the Brown Scapular of Carmel. Cling to these weapons against Satan.

May 9, 1990

Message:
My children, when the Cross is erected on the hill and our Holy Project is completed, I desire that once a year on the Feast of St. Francis, that you bring your animals to the hill to be blessed. St. Francis loved the animals and so do I.

Your prayers, penances, praise and obedience are spiritual stones on which your new chapel will be built. These stones are cemented together by the power of the Holy Spirit and my intercessions, so the chapel in each of your hearts will be united for the cause of the building of the chapel on the hill of peace.

May 10, 1990

MESSAGE:

My children, I wish for you to have a special effusion of the gift of understanding so the Holy Spirit will enlighten you in His truths.

Pray for the United States. Pray that materialism and every form of evil vanish from the United States. The United states is dear to me and I intend to protect the nation and keep it "One Nation Under God."

My children, your life is what you make of it. You were given a free will because my Son desires for you to love and follow Him freely in love. Since you have control over your free will, you can make your life a "little Heaven upon earth," by following Jesus and me, or a "little hell upon earth," by choosing evil. What will you choose for your life?

May 11, 1990

MESSAGE:

My children, when you go to Confession, go with a good disposition. Really be sorry for your sins and truly resolve to never commit your sins again. When you confess your sins you should have a deep inner peace and relief.

Have no double values in your life. Do not try to be good but let parts of your life be evil. Come all the way to my Heart without fear. Relinquish evil and all double standards of living. Imitate the poverty of St. Francis. St. Francis was the saint who led a life most like Jesus. Be poor and humble in spirit.

My children I am very concerned about the idea of your raising monetary funds for the undertakings of the Cross project. Consider that this could turn people away from the project and away from Jesus and me. Trust that this same money you want to raise will be taken care of by voluntary donation — by persons who just give freely without your raising funds...

I desire that when the chapel is erected on the hill of peace, that you have a small booklet written and published about all the history of the founding and building of this chapel. This chapel will be a religious and historical memorial.

Let not one of you remain in spiritual darkness. I have the power to bring any sinner through the tunnel of the darkness, of sin and evil, into the Light of Holiness, Peace, Joy and Love which is Jesus. This power is a power of intercession. I am simply your interceding Mother who always submits humbly to His Will. He knows that I do not ask any favors which are not for the good of your souls, so He is eager to grant my requests.

May 12, 1990

MESSAGE:
My children, be good listeners. Do not always have to get in the last word. There are beautiful spiritual

lessons to be learned from listening to the other person. Do not think that you know it all and can't learn from someone else.

May 13, 1990

MESSAGE:
My children, I am like a deep well holding all the graces and mercy needed. This well has a supply of the waters of salvation which will never run dry. All of you need my graces and mercy, and must not restrain from coming to receive them. The supply of water for this well is in My Immaculate Heart. This well is easily reached. When the bucket is dropped into the waters of My Heart, you receive all you need. Come to this full well and receive the graces for salvation.

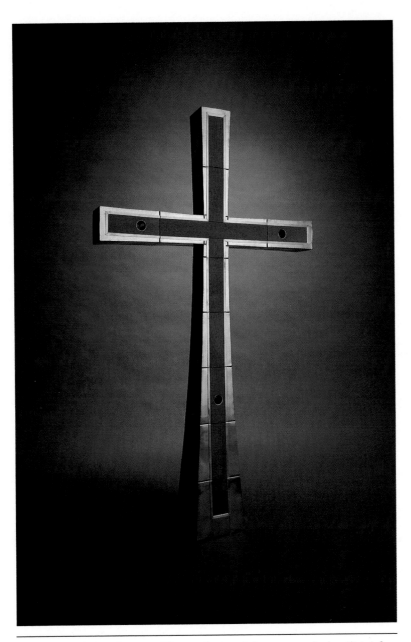

Model of the Cross - The scale model was made by Patrick Shelton and Mackey Real of Santa Maria.

Barbara Matthias during ecstasy.

Father René Laurentin consults with Dr. Charles Yingling and Dr. Linda Davenport after reviewing results of scientific tests.

Father René Laurentin and Anna Marie Maagdenberg MSN, NP part of the medical team and Suzanne Shutte- One of the translators discuss the medical testing.

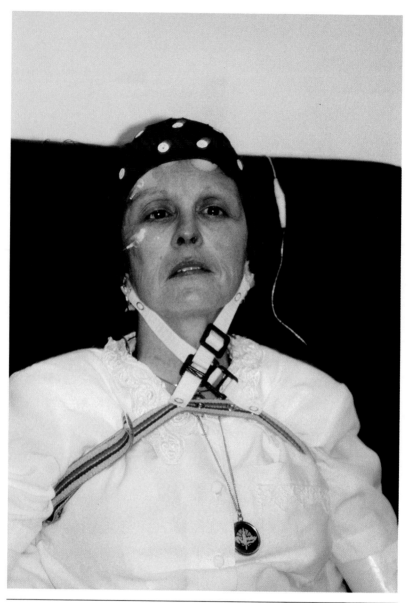
Barbara Matthias during testing.

Dr. Robert Levenson of U.C. Berkley explaining tests to Barbara.

Msgr. John W. Rhode observes testing session by investigators.

Barbara Matthias during an Apparition at the Marion Hospital Chapel in Santa Maria.

Original Santa Maria prayer group mentioned in early chapter of this book.

The Author and Fr. René Laurentin review facts for this book.

The site chosen by Our Lady for the Cross.

Fr. René Laurentin and Dr. Philippe Loron interview Barbara at her apartment.

Barbara Matthias during ecstasy.